EXPLORING THE REACHES OF THE SOLAR SYSTEM

SPACE EXPLORATION

EXPLORING THE REACHES OF THE SOLAR SYSTEM

Ray Spangenburg and Diane Moser

Facts On File

New York • Oxford • Sydney

To all the pioneers and voyagers—
men, women and machines—
who for all humankind
probe the unknown, ask questions and seek answers . . .

and in memory of Lindy,
whose pride and courage remained true to the end.

Exploring the Reaches of the Solar System

Copyright © 1990 by Ray Spangenburg and Diane Moser

Facts On File, Inc.
460 Park Avenue South
New York NY 10016
USA

Facts On File Limited
Collins Street
Oxford OX4 1XJ
United Kingdom

Facts On File Pty Ltd
Talavera & Khartoum Rds
North Ryde NSW 2113
Australia

Library of Congress Cataloging-in-Publication Data
Spangenburg, Ray, 1939-
    Space exploration : exploring the reaches of the solar system /
Ray Spangenburg and Diane Moser.
      p. cm.
    Summary: Discusses the exploration of stars and planets within our solar system including the 1976 Viking landing on Mars and the Voyager explorations of Saturn, Jupiter, Uranus, and Neptune.
    Includes bibliographical references.
    ISBN 0-8160-1850-2
    1. Planets—Exploration. 2. Solar System—Exploration.
[1. Planets—Exploration. 2. Solar system—Exploration.]
I. Moser, Diane, 1944- . II. Title.
QB601.S683 1990
919.9'204—dc20   89-37711

British and Australian CIP data available on request from Facts On File.

Text and Jacket design by Ron Monteleone
Composition by Facts On File, Inc.
Manufactured by Maple-Vail Book Manufacturing Group
Printed in the United States of America

10 9 8 7 6 5 4 3 2 1

This book is printed on acid-free paper.

CONTENTS

PREFACE

As the 21st century draws near, we stand at the brink of a vast new frontier, with new keys to age-old mysteries of the universe within our grasp. Our understanding of our place in it grows with each new piece of data we receive from the far-flung robot eyes of spacecraft like Voyager, Galileo and Magellan, and will continue to grow as future craft spin endlessly through infinite space.

Exploring the Reaches of the Solar System takes a look at the way space-age technology has advanced our understanding of this universe we live in. Part One begins with space-age explorations of the inner planets and their satellites, including Mercury, Venus, our own Moon and Mars. From there we move outward in Part Two to the fascinating ring and satellite systems of the gaseous giants Jupiter and Saturn, and further to Uranus, Neptune and Pluto. Part Three of our tour looks at the most familiar planet, our Earth, examines our non-planetary neighbors, the asteroids and comets, and finishes with the stars, focusing first on our own Sun, and then, moving outward, on the galaxies, nebulas, dwarf stars, quasars, pulsars and more that lie beyond.

Other books in this series tell other parts of the saga with: the story of the first space scientists, test pilots, and early astronauts and cosmonauts, including the Apollo missions to the Moon (*Opening the Space Frontier*); the adventure and challenge of developing space as a livable workplace and putting space to work for humankind (*Living and Working in Space*); and close-ups of the lives of space pioneers from the beginning to the present (*Space People from A-Z*).

Together these books tell an exciting tale of human intelligence at its best—dreaming dreams, solving problems and achieving results. Today's world owes much to those who gave their work and their lives in the past and to those who venture today—both personally, in manned programs, and intellectually, through their work—into space.

ACKNOWLEDGMENTS

This book could never have happened without the help of countless individuals in both industry and government throughout the world. While we won't try to name them all, we appreciate the time so many took to provide photographs, drawings and information. A few stand out as extraordinary, and to them a special "thank you": Michael Drake, of the Lunar and Planetary Laboratory at the University of Arizona, for taking time to read the manuscript and make many helpful suggestions for clarity and accuracy; astronomer William K. Hartmann and Wadsworth Publishing Company for use of diagrams from his work *Astronomy: The Cosmic Journey*, 2nd ed.; Christopher P. McKay, exobiologist and planetary scientist at NASA's Ames Research Center, for his many discussions with us that contributed both directly and indirectly to this work; Harold P. Klein, formerly of the Viking Imaging Team; Michael H. Carr of the U.S. Geological Survey; Lelia Coyne and Joe Pinto of NASA Ames; and Bill Hartmann all for taking time to discuss their work with us. Thanks for help on the artwork to Jurrie J. van der Woude of JPL and Alan Barnard of Graphic Hobby House in Sacramento. Also our thanks to four magazine editors who have given us a steady stream of fascinating assignments on space over the years: Tony Reichhardt of *Final Frontier*, John Rhea, formerly of *Space World*, and Kate McMains and Leonard David of *Ad Astra*. For their supportive enthusiasm, our thanks to our agent Linda Allen and to James Warren and Deirdre Mullane, our editors at Facts On File. Also at Facts On File, our appreciation to Kathy Ishizuka for her patience and organizational powers; Michael Laraque for a fine job of copyediting; Ron Monteleone for creating an outstanding design; and Erik Ehn and Terri Dieli for a difficult production job well done. And our very special thanks for spirited late-night talk and steady encouragement throughout the years to Laurie Wise—scientist, humanitarian and friend. Without you all this book would not be.

INTRODUCTION:

THE BIRTH OF THE SOLAR SYSTEM

We shall not cease from exploration
And the end of all our exploring
Will be to arrive where we started
And know the place for the first time.
—T. S. Eliot

Searching out the mysteries of the universe, asking questions and seeking answers—in the known universe, humankind alone pursues these quests. It's a giant concept—the universe—mind-boggling in its dimensions. Each night as we see the black sky fill with tiny lights, it is difficult to imagine that the nearest star is over 25 trillion miles away and that light traveling from that star, speeding at 186,000 miles a second, has traveled a distance of over 4.3 light years to reach us. That star, Proxima Centauri, one of the two stars in the Alpha Centauri binary star system, is only one of nearly 3,000 stars visible in our sky without a telescope. Observation with telescopes has shown us that many more groups of stars—galaxies of them—fill the universe. In fact the universe contains many *billions* of galaxies, each in turn containing many billions of stars.

One small galaxy that we call the Milky Way is home to the star we call the Sun. The Sun is only one of the many millions of stars that make up the Milky Way galaxy. It is, however, *our* star, the source of our warmth, of our days and nights, the centerpiece of our infinitesimally small portion of the great blackness of the universe, the vast unknown.

Present theory holds that the Sun, Earth, and the eight other planets of our Solar System were formed a little over 4.5 billion years ago by the contraction of a giant cloud (the primeval nebula) of interstellar gas composed mainly of hydrogen, helium and particles of dust. The exact trigger that began this contraction is not well understood, but some scientists believe that it may have started when shock waves from a nearby supernova, or stellar explosion, rippled through space, upsetting the delicate balance of the loose cloud's original state. Whatever the cause, once the process started, the contraction continued under the natural and inevitable force of the gravitational attraction within the cloud itself. Contracting and spinning violently, the cloud became disk-shaped and flattened around its outer edges. Meanwhile the huge ball of matter that collected in its center contracted into a heavier and heavier mass to become the developing Sun.

As the cloud continued to spin more and more rapidly, its billions of small particles of dust began to collide with greater violence and frequency, concentrating in the plane of the disk. Gradually these grains built up into larger and larger chunks. And as these "planetesimals," early ancestors of the planets and their satellites, reached a certain size, they no longer dependedonly upon accidental collision to expand their mass. Instead they began to build up enough mass to use gravity to reach out and attract more and more particles of solid material. These "protoplanets" gradually accreted and built up, most of them continuing to rotate and revolve following the direction of the parent nebula from which they were born.

Meanwhile, although the gigantic mass of the slowly developing and contracting Sun had not yet begun to kick on its nuclear furnace, the temperatures in the inner Solar System were high enough to keep volatile substances like water, methane and ammonia in a gaseous state. Thus, the inner planets (known as "terrestrials" because they are more Earth-like) formed from such nonvolatile components of the nebula as iron and silicates. But out further from the embryo Sun, the lower temperatures allowed the volatiles to become incorporated into the formation of the giant outer planets, at the same time allowing these giants to expand by attracting and gathering large quantities of light elements like hydrogen and helium from the surrounding nebula.

As the Sun continued to collapse and the density and temperature in the inner core began to rise, it approached a critical temperature of around 10 million degrees Kelvin and began to generate energy by the nuclear fusion of hydrogen. Once switched on, the Sun also began to generate a solar wind, a flow of electrically charged particles, and like a giant leaf-blower began driving the remaining gas and dust grains out of the Solar System.

Meanwhile, heated by their accretional energy and internal radioactivity, the cores of the protoplanets began to melt, forming the internal structure the planets still have today. Finally, the remaining planetesimals, those too heavy to be swept away by the solar wind, began to blast the developing planets—during a great half-billion-year bombardment whose impact scars can still be seen today on most of the planets.

PART 1

EXPLORING THE INNER PLANETS

1

MERCURY: NEXT-DOOR TO THE SUN

Mercury's surface could not be observed [by early astronomers] because of the planet's small size, its distance from the Earth, and closeness to the Sun . . . .
Our shiny, fragile spacecraft have given us a perspective totally unavailable to the greatest scientists of the past.
—James A. Dunne and Eric Burgess
in *The Voyage of Mariner 10*

The surface of Mercury records the early history of the cataclysmic events that occurred during the formation of our solar system. The primordial state of the planet's surface, when studied in combination with . . . the Moon and Mars, should provide a great step forward in our understanding of the origin and evolution of the solar system and thus of our planet Earth.
—John E. Naugle, Chief Scientist, NASA

Like a tiny moth circling a bright and beckoning light, the planet Mercury wings closest of all to the Sun. Darting swiftly along its elliptical path, it defies the optical mirrors of our telescopes and quickly escapes our curious gaze with its forays close to its too-bright neighbor the Sun. Its surface parched by billions of years on this course, Mercury hangs poised, it seems, on the brink of fiery disaster.

No fluttering moth, however, Mercury is in reality a heavy mass of rock and iron baking in the Sun's blazing heat. Completing its tortuous journey around the Sun once every 88 Earth days, at an average distance of only 58 million miles from the solar furnace, Mercury is one of the most difficult planets of all to observe from Earth. Never more than 28 degrees from the Sun in the sky, as seen from Earth, we can view it only for a very short time in the morning and evening. In fact in ancient times Mercury, like Venus, was thought to be two different stars. The Greek astronomers called the morning appearance Apollo and the evening planet's visitation Hermes (the Greek name for the god Mercury).

Even the invention of the telescope did little to bring Mercury into better focus. Its tiny size (only 3,031 miles, or 4,878 km in diameter), and its proximity to the Sun make visual study difficult. Although some maps of the planet were attempted as early as the end of the 19th century, most were

Mercury: The Planet

Position: Closest to Sun

Average Distance from Sun: 36 million miles (57.9 million km)—compared to Earth at 92.95 billion miles (149.59 million km)

Diameter: 3,031 miles (4,878 km), 38% the size of Earth

Mass: 0.055 times Earth's

Density: 5.43 (Water = 1)

Volume: 0.56 times Earth's

Surface Gravity: 0.377 times Earth's

Period of Rotation on Axis: Once every 58.65 Earth days

Revolution around Sun: Once every 87.97 Earth days (sidereal period); 115.88 days as seen from Earth

Orbital Speed: 29.7 miles/sec (47.8 km/sec)

Satellites: None

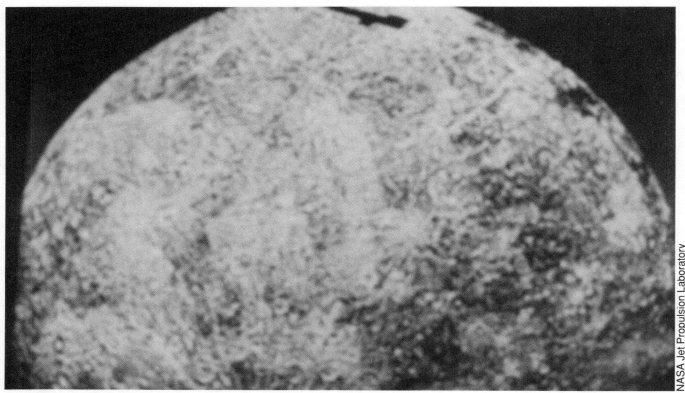

NASA Jet Propulsion Laboratory

Mariner 10 view of Mercury

sketchy and inaccurate. For a long time, too, many astronomers believed that Mercury, like the Moon, took equal time to rotate on its axis and to complete one orbital revolution—since it always seemed to keep the same face turned toward the Earth. We now know that this is wrong and that the planet is locked by the Sun's gravitational effect into a 59-day period of rotation about its axis—only about two-thirds of its

88-day trip around the Sun. This means that the movement of the Sun across Mercury's sky would appear agonizingly slow and would take about 176 Earth days to go from one Mercury noon to the next. Because of its combination of slow rotation and fast orbit there are approximately one-and-one-third Mercury days (or complete rotations) in every Mercury year! Christmas morning would never be more than a day-and-a-third away on Mercury, but a school day (or any other day) would seem to last forever!

Today's astronomers have studied and partially mapped Mercury by bouncing radar beams from Earth-based telescopes off its surface, but the only space mission so far to the innermost planet has been the very successful U.S. space probe called Mariner 10. A brilliantly conceived probe launched to examine the two innermost planets, Mercury and Venus, Mariner 10 was the first to use a gravity assist technique to reach its destination. Launched on November 3, 1973, it flew past Venus in early February 1974. Then, using Venus's gravitational field to whip it around and gain extra energy—something like being spun around and then released from a carnival ride—it encountered Mercury in late March 1974. Especially fitted out with protection against solar radiation, Mariner 10 flew within 437 miles (703 km) of Mercury's surface. Carrying two television cameras with 4.92-ft (1.5-m) telescopes, an x-band radio transmitter, infrared radiometer, and equipment for ultraviolet experimentation, it transmitted nearly 2,500 pictures back to Earth. After zipping across the Mercury sky, the spacecraft then flew into an orbit around the Sun that was designed to cross Mercury's path again, in a kind of celestial ambush allowing more encounters. Unfortunately, only two more photo sessions were planned, but after those were taken in September 1974 and March 1975, with over 3,000 more pictures sent back to Earth, scientists at last had a better understanding of the Sun's closest neighbor.

Space-Age Mercury

As the first pictures came in from Mercury, scientists were struck by the planet's close resemblance to the Moon. From the evidence strewn across its parched and pitted surface, they concluded that Mercury's geological history may have been similar in many ways to our own lunar companion's. Like the Moon, Mercury is scarred and pock-marked by thousands of craters formed by meteorite impacts millions of years ago.

In fact, though, the Moon actually has more flat and open areas known as *maria* or "seas" than Mercury

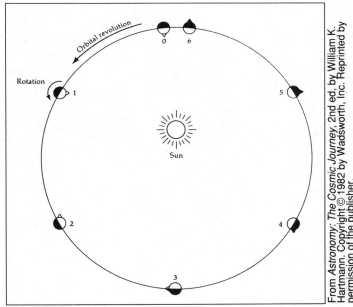

This cartoon of the planet Mercury shows the relationship between its rotation and its revolution. As the planet moves counterclockwise through its orbital revolution around the Sun, from positions 0 through 6, an imaginary high mountain sketched on its surface serves as a marker for its rotation (also counterclockwise, around its own internal axis). At position 0, a person standing on the mountain would see the Sun shining directly overhead (noontime). (The shaded area indicates the nighttime side of the planet.) The planet has completed its rotation, with the mountain back facing in the same position, at position 4, two-thirds of the way around the Sun. At position 6 it is midnight at the mountain. It will take another complete revolution around the Sun (positions 7 through 12, not shown), or 88 more Earth days, to bring the mountain back to a position where the Sun is once again directly overhead. To go from noon to noon at that point on the planet's surface has taken 176 Earth days, two full revolutions of Mercury around the Sun.

From Astronomy: The Cosmic Journey, 2nd ed, by William K. Hartmann. Copyright © 1982 by Wadsworth, Inc. Reprinted by permission of the publisher.

has. With the exception of one gigantic flat area known as the Caloris Basin and a few other small patches, Mercury is almost entirely cratered. And, while scientists believe that the Moon's maria were created by lava flows, most hold an entirely different theory about the formation of Caloris Basin. Although some evidence points to past volcanic activity on the planet, including some partial infilling of the basin itself, the Caloris Basin was probably formed by the most dramatic and important event in Mercury's long history.

Evidence suggests that an asteroid—possibly measuring over 60 miles (97 km) across—collided long ago with the tiny world and leveled an area nearly 850 miles (1,400 km) across. As it smashed into Mercury at the speed of over 315,000 miles per hour

(507,000 kph), this huge interplanetary "missile" forever changed the face of the planet, pushing up mountain ranges over a mile-and-a-half high around the rim of the crater it formed. Even the confused, jumbled surface on the opposite side of the globe may also have been created by the collision of the impact's gigantic shock waves as they circled the planet.

Besides being the major geological event in Mercury's history, the Caloris Basin impact may have also been the last important event in the planet's evolution. Judging from crust fractures and other evidence, Mercury had apparently shrunk substantially prior to that impact, possibly through either a cooling of the iron core or a slowing of the planet's spin. Mercury's battered surface now suggests that after its initial bombardment by space debris, followed briefly by what may have been a period of volcanic activity, the planet then ceased to evolve. Although some small ridges, cracks and other features hint that there may have been some further tectonic activity linked to changes in the planet's interior, for the most part Mercury "died" at the end of the same great bombardment that devastated the Moon, some 3.9 billion years ago.

Incredibly inhospitable to life, Mercury has an atmosphere so thin that it might be described as almost a perfect vacuum, with temperatures ranging (for lack of an atmospheric blanket) on the average from such extremes as 440 degrees F (227 degrees C) at noon to −279 degrees F (−173 degrees C) at night. It is doubtful that humankind will ever set foot on Mercury's surface. Unshielded by atmosphere and clouds and awash in dangerous ultraviolet rays emanating from the Sun, Mercury will always remain a truly alien planet.

Mercury's Mysteries—Hidden in the Glare of the Sun

The first and only mission to Mercury, Mariner 10 gave scientists many clues to the planet's past, but some mysteries still remain. Because of its complex trajectory and schedule, Mariner 10 viewed the same hemisphere of the planet in each of its three visits. While we don't expect the planet's other hemisphere to hold any major surprises, differences in the Moon's hemispheres suggest there may still be some interesting new observations awaiting us on Mercury as well.

For a planet only about 40% the size of Earth, Mercury has a remarkably strong gravitational pull, due to its surprisingly massive, high-density iron core. So large in fact that scientists maintain it must make up nearly 80% of the entire planet's mass! If this

Mariner 10 spacecraft

NASA Jet Propulsion Laboratory

is true, then the core of Mercury alone would be larger than Earth's Moon. Exactly how and when Mercury formed such a large core remains unclear.

Adding to this mystery is the presence of Mercury's magnetic field, puzzling even though it's only about 1% the force of the Earth's. Since rapid rotation of a molten iron core usually acts as the generator for such a field, how could a planet that spins nearly 60 times slower than Earth produce even a small magnetic field? And how could such a small planet have preserved a molten core into the present era? Most theorists think it should have solidified long, long ago. Could the magnetic field actually be a "fossil" left over from the planet's early history, as some scientists believe? Or could it perhaps result from some unknown interaction between the planet and the Sun's magnetic field?

Sailing into the Future

These questions remain unanswered. Yet no planned missions to Mercury lie ahead, and even future Earth-based telescopes will no doubt have difficulty distinguishing the planet from its hiding place next to the Sun. Even the launching in 1990 of the

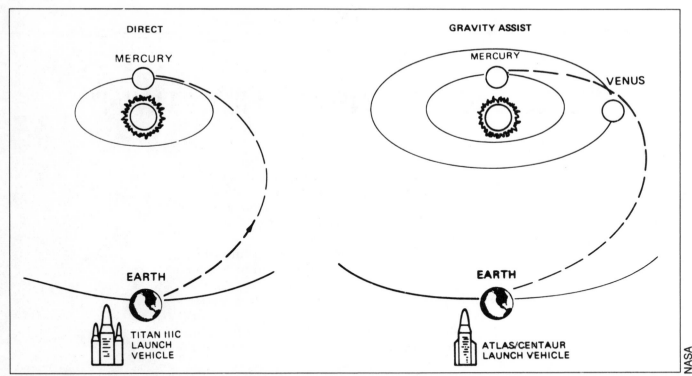

Gravity assist to Mercury via Venus. Mercury 10 made use of the gravity and orbital motion of Venus to boost the spacecraft on its way into the inner Solar System. Using this "slingshot" boost, NASA could launch Mariner 10 with a much smaller launch vehicle than a direct flight to Mercury would have required

Hubble Space Telescope, a remarkable instrument that will revolutionize astronomy, will be of little help with Mercury—since the orbiting telescope is programmed to face away from the planet in order to protect its very valuable instruments from the Sun.

Interested scientists and engineering firms have promoted "unofficial" ideas for future missions to Mercury, though, and the most intriguing of those is a proposal for a solar-sail mission to the evasive planet. Instead of battling the Sun's destructive forces, a solar-sail mission would use the Sun's own energy to actually push against a "sail" of thin aluminum film. Like a sailboat capturing the wind for its propulsion, the economical solar-sail craft would use the Sun's rays to "sail" to its destination and release a tiny explorer probe.

For the time being, though, scientists hoping to unlock Mercury's secrets are limited to sorting through the mountains of data collected during the Mariner 10 mission and by Earth-based radar mapping. While this work may help us to further understand many of the the planet's mysteries, without further space missions it's unlikely that Mercury's major secrets will be unlocked anytime soon.

Meanwhile, the stalwart Mariner 10 continues to pass close to Mercury every few months but no longer has the power to take clear photographs or send them back for us to see. Out of the gas needed to point the craft, it now orbits on in space, lonely and isolated from its makers.

2

VENUS: OUR UNEARTHLY "TWIN"

Venus appears to offer roasting heat, a choking atmosphere, crushing pressure, and murky skies, to which forbidding weather and hostile terrain may perhaps be added.
—technical memorandum from the Mariner 5 team

Some have spent more than ten years laboriously and methodically developing instruments that return but one hour of scientific data! But what an hour. Few people get as much return in a lifetime.
—Lawrence Colin in The Planets (1985, Bantam)

At the surface a dim, peachy light filters through the thick Venusian clouds of deadly sulfuric acid. Gentle breezes stir the intense 891 degrees F (477 degrees C) heat of the barren, dusty high-plains desert, while 217-mile-per-hour (350 kph) winds in the upper atmosphere whip clouds overhead 60 times faster than the strange backward rotation of the planet. In the distance, perhaps, turbulent flashes of lightning brighten the sky around the conic shape of a volcano spewing out smoke and ash.

If human beings could survive on such a hostile planet at all, even a brief walk on its surface would require the protection of heavy, air-conditioned pressure suits. Lumbering awkwardly through the dense surface atmosphere, visiting astronauts would labor under the enormous weight of atmospheric pressure 95 times that on Earth.

In fact, it's unlikely that human beings will ever walk on the inhospitable surface of the planet Venus, second from the Sun. But between 1962 and 1985 our

"ambassadors" did go there—nearly two dozen times. Both the U.S. and the Soviet Union sent highly mechanized robot searchers to probe the atmosphere, parachute to the surface, or watch from orbit, scooping out the facts from the dense, murky soup of clouds. One more, called Magellan, set off for Venus in 1989. Meanwhile, from the Earth, new radar observation techniques have yielded fresh data. As a result, the past 25 years have brought enormous insights about our mysterious neighbor.

The "Mystery Planet"
Brightly gleaming in the early morning or early evening sky, Venus caught the attention of ancient skywatchers as far back as 3000 B.C., when the Babylonians recorded its movements across the sky. Much later, Galileo's telescope, newly invented in 1610, discovered that like the Moon the shrouded planet went through phases—from a crescent to a full circle, and back. That's when Galileo realized that

Venus: The Planet

Position: Second from Sun
Average Distance from Sun: 67.19 million miles (108 million km)—compared to Earth at 92.95 million miles (149.59 million km)
Diameter: 7,519 miles (12,100 km), 95% the size of Earth
Mass: 0.82 times Earth's
Density: 5.24 (Water = 1)
Volume: 0.86 times Earth's
Surface Gravity: 0.91 times Earth's
Period of Rotation on Axis: Once every 243 Earth days, east to west
Revolution around Sun: Once every 224.7 Earth days (sidereal period)
Orbital Speed: 21.7 miles/sec (35 km/sec)
Satellites: None

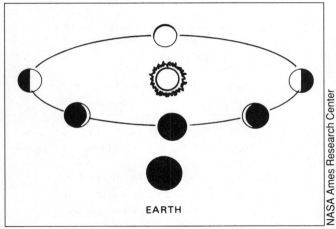

EARTH

In 1610 Galileo first discovered that Venus has phases like Earth's Moon

NASA Ames Research Center

NASA Ames Research Center

A view of Venusian clouds as seen by the Pioneer Venus Orbiter

Venusian light, like the light of the Moon, was actually a reflection of the Sun's rays.

At the only time when Venus is really observable from Earth—when it passes closest to us—it always turns the same side toward us, leaving the other side completely hidden. Even though astronomical observatories developed more and more powerful optical telescopes, a thick veil of Venusian clouds continued to block our view revealing only a bright white haze that no one could see through.

The presence of those clouds led astronomers, planetologists and science-fiction writers to extensive speculations. Maybe Venus was a rainy, tropical planet, with seas and jungles teeming with life. We couldn't see the surface—but, one assumption went, surely clouds meant water vapor and water vapor probably meant life. Closest to Earth both in distance (only 26 million miles, or 42 million km, away) and in size (with diameter, mass, and density nearly the same as Earth's), for a long time Venus seemed like Earth's twin, a remarkably good home for extraterrestrial life.

That idea died out slowly. New astronomical techniques invented in the early 1930s—radiometry and spectroscopy—began to give the first hints about its inhospitable atmospheric composition and temperature. By 1961, microwave astronomy gave us further insights about the planet's direction and rate of rotation, atmospheric temperature, density and pressure, and a rough idea of topography. But only with the first planetary missions and Mariner 2's successful flyby in 1962 did we begin to confirm fully how unlike Earth Venus really is.

Sending Robot Eyes and Sensors to Venus

With the advent of the space age, our neighbor Venus naturally became one of the first planetary goals. As early as February 4, 1961, the Soviets launched Sputnik 7 from a platform in Earth orbit—possibly to probe Venus, although it may have been just a test flight, as it descended back to Earth 21 days later. Soon on its heels followed another Soviet spacecraft, Venera 1, launched on February 12, but ground communica-

Unveiling Venus: U.S. and Soviet Missions Since 1961

1961 **Venera 1 USSR** Launched February 12 by Sputnik 8, the spacecraft passed within 62,000 miles (99,800 km) of the planet but lost radio contact with Earth before arrival. First Soviet planetary mission.

1962 **Mariner 1 U.S.** Launched July 22, this craft was destroyed before reaching orbit for safety reasons.

* **Mariner 2 U.S.** This interplanetary flyby, launched on August 27, encountered Venus on December 14. It passed within 21,603 miles (34,766 km) of Venus to give us the first close-up data, revealing 800 degree F (427 degree C) surface temperatures and no magnetic field.

1964 **Zond 1 USSR** Although this flyby, launched April 2, passed Venus at approximately 62,000 miles (100,000 km), communications failed en route. Spacecraft continued into solar orbit.

1965 **Venera 2 USSR** Launched November 12, the spacecraft passed close to Venus (about 15,000 miles, 24,000 km) on February 27, 1966, but returned no data because of communications problems.

* **Venera 3 USSR** Intended to execute a soft-landing on Venus, the Venera 3 spacecraft was launched on November 16 and crashed on the Venusian surface on March 1, 1966, becoming the first man-made object to impact another planet. However, it failed to transmit data.

1967 * **Venera 4 USSR** Launched June 12, this spacecraft carried an instrumented capsule that descended by parachute through the atmosphere of Venus on October 18, returning data for 94 minutes, including a temperature reading of 536 degrees F (280 degrees C).

* **Mariner 5 U.S.** Launched June 14, this flyby mission established that 72½ to 87½% of the planet's atmosphere is made up of carbon dioxide. Mariner 5 passed within 2,480 miles (3,991 km) on October 19.

1969 * **Venera 5 USSR** This probe, launched on January 5, transmitted atmospheric measurements and other planetary data as it braked through the atmosphere on May 16, confirming a high carbon dioxide content and no water vapor.

* **Venera 6 USSR** Launched on January 10, this probe arrived on Venus on May 17 successfully duplicating the Venera 5 mission.

1970 * **Venera 7 USSR** In the first soft-landing on another planet, this spacecraft was launched on August 17 and descended by parachute—repeating Venera 5 and 6 experiments—to touch down on the surface December 15 and transmit for 23 minutes.

* Indicates a successful mission

1972   *** Venera 8   USSR**   Launched March 27, Venera 8 executed a successful soft-landing on the sunlit surface of Venus on July 22. It survived on the surface for 50 minutes, long enough to report back temperatures of more than 752 degrees F (400 degrees C) and pressure readings 90 times the Earth's.

1973   **Mariner 10   U.S.**   Encountering Venus on February 5, 1974, this mission was launched on November 3, 1973, collecting data on the atmosphere, environment and surface of Venus. As it flew by and continued on to Mercury, Mariner 10's 3,712 photos of Venus at 328-foot (100 m) resolution proved 7,000 times better than those taken from Earth.

1975   ***Venera 9, Venera 10   USSR**   June 8 and 14 launches sent these back-to-back exploration vehicles to land on Venus on October 22 and 25. They sent back the first pictures ever transmitted from the surface of another planet, showing us the rocky plains of Venus, plus the results of atmospheric analyses, a temperature reading of 905 degrees F (485 degrees C) and other data.

1978   *** Pioneer Venus 1   U.S.**   (Pioneer 12)   Launched on May 20, this spacecraft became the first Venus orbiter, beginning on December 4. Its detailed radar mapping of the planet's surface discovered rift valleys and the 7-mile-high Maxwell Montes. The mission also studied the interaction between the Venusian atmosphere and the solar wind. Still orbiting, the spacecraft was turned to observe passing comets in 1984 and 1986.

   * Pioneer Venus Multiprobe   U.S.   (Pioneer Venus 2 or Pioneer 13)   The second vehicle in the Pioneer Venus program, Pioneer 13 was launched August 8 and split into four atmospheric probes (and a bus) on arrival December 9. They obtained temperature and pressure readings, plus data on wind patterns.

Artist's concept of Pioneer Venus Orbiter above the clouds of Venus

NASA Ames Research Center

Venera 11   USSR   This flyby-lander combination, launched September 9 and arriving December 25, sent a descent vehicle to soft-land, detecting thunder and lightning in the atmosphere. The flyby portion of the mission acted as a relay station for communications.

Venera 12   USSR   Similar to Venera 11, this flyby-lander was launched September 14, arriving December 21. It also collected useful surface and atmosphere data, but returned no photos.

1981   Venera 13   USSR   Launched October 30, this orbiter-lander touched down on March 3, 1982 and sent back the first color pictures of the Venusian surface, operating on the surface for 127 minutes.

Venera 14   USSR   On March 5, 1982, the lander portion of this orbiter-lander mission, launched November 4, 1981, sent back color imagery, drilled soil samples and conducted seismic experimentation. From its landing site 590 miles (950 km) southeast of the Venera 13 site, it sent back information for 57 minutes.

1983   Venera 15   USSR   This orbiter, launched June 2, arrived October 10 and produced radar mapping with .6 to 1.2 mile (1 to 2 km) resolution, including the poles.

Venera 16   USSR   With a June 7 launch date and an October 16 arrival date, this orbiter, like Venera 15, conducted radar mapping, plus atmospheric analyses.

1984   * VEGA 1, VEGA 2   USSR   The back-to-back Venus-Comet Halley missions—launched December 15 and 21 respectively—carried Venus descent vehicles, atmospheric balloon probes and numerous multinational experiment packages, descending June 10-11 (VEGA 1) and June 14-15 (VEGA 2), 1985. Both flyby vehicles continued on to rendezvous successfully with Comet Halley in March 1986.

1989   Magellan   U.S.   An orbiter mission launched on the Space Shuttle in April 1989, the Magellan radar mapper is equipped to provide the best combination of high-resolution pictures and thorough coverage of Venus to date.

1991   Vesta   USSR   A multiple-asteroid mission, planned to take a gravity assist at Venus, dropping off a lander on the surface of the planet to photograph and make seismic measurements.

---

tions lost touch soon afterward, spoiling this effort. The Soviets would continue to lob other spacecraft toward Venus for another four years without encouraging results, but their persistent interest in the veiled planet would pay off in the end.

Meanwhile, early American efforts also sputtered when their first planetary mission to Venus, Mariner 1, developed a fatal guidance problem in July 1962.

Mariner 2

When back-up Mariner 2 veered skyward a month later, on August 27, 1962, once again the Atlas guidance system hiccupped, but this time, luckily, the problem was not so severe. Mariner smoothed out into Earth orbit, received a boost from its upper-stage rocket, and set off on a new path. The first successful interplanetary flight was on its way to Venus.

Designed at NASA's Jet Propulsion Laboratory (JPL), the stalwart little Mariner 2 craft measured only 12 feet (3.65 m) high and sported a pair of solar cell panels that gave it a total width of 16.5 feet (5.03 m). As Mariner 2 glided through space, some of the 40 scientific instruments on board began their work—measuring the strength of the magnetic field between Earth and Venus, registering the flux of high-energy cosmic rays, and detecting particles between the two worlds.

One of the most exciting discoveries made en route was verification of the solar wind. Astronomers had observed for a long time that a comet's tail, or coda,

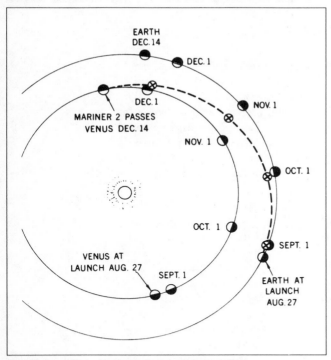

EARTH
DEC. 14

DEC. 1

DEC. 1

MARINER 2 PASSES
VENUS DEC. 14

NOV. 1

NOV. 1

OCT. 1

OCT. 1

SEPT. 1

VENUS AT
LAUNCH AUG. 27

SEPT. 1

EARTH AT
LAUNCH
AUG. 27

The flight path to Venus taken by Mariner 2

streams away from the Sun—no matter which direction the comet is moving. First detected in 1960 by Pioneer 5, which studied solar energy, the solar wind is the flow of charged particles—mostly protons and electrons—streaming outward from the Sun's corona at supersonic speeds. Mariner 2 positively confirmed the presence of this ionized gas of particles blowing at speeds from 185 to 500 miles per second (300-800 km/sec)—up to nearly 2 million mph (more than 3 million kph)!

By December 14, Mariner 2 had arrived. The little craft flew first on the night side and then on the sunlit side of the planet, approaching within about 21,600 miles (34,760 km) of the Venusian surface, and moving at a rate of about 87,890 mph (141,440 kph).

On arrival, the magnetometer confirmed what many scientists had already suspected: Unlike Earth, Venus had virtually no magnetic field. In addition, Mariner 2 reported, no radiation belt surrounded the planet. The Earth, by contrast, has radiation belts (the Van Allen Radiation Region), which were first discovered by early U.S. Explorer satellites in 1958—probably created, scientists believe, by Earth's capture of energetic particles by its magnetic field. The news from Mariner 2 at Venus helped confirm this idea, since Venus, scientists now knew, had neither a magnetic field nor any radiation belt!

Mariner 2, and the spacecraft that would follow, supported the new picture of Venus that had begun to evolve out of new techniques in ground-based astronomy. Very unlike Earth's, Venus's atmosphere turns out to be almost entirely carbon dioxide (96%), while our planet's is 77% nitrogen and 21% oxygen. Small amounts of nitrogen, water vapor, and sulfur dioxide, with even smaller traces of a few other gases, were also found in the atmosphere surrounding Venus. Later observations, in 1975, proved that the heavy vapor was not water, but searing sulfuric acid. In addition, the clouds contain other highly corrosive compounds such as hydrofluoric and hydrochloric acid.

Everyone was curious about the temperature on Venus, but Mariner 2 carried no surface probes. Whatever it would discover, it would have to detect from a distance of 21,600 miles, but its microwave radiometer could test for surface temperature and confirmed Earth-based tests, showing a sweltering 800 degrees F (427 degrees C)—hot enough to melt lead—both on the night and day sides of the planet. Meanwhile, understandably, no water vapor at all was detected.

The high surface temperature fit in with the high concentration of carbon dioxide, whose heat-trapping abilities produced a furnace-like "greenhouse effect" (see box). Combined with the ocean-like weight of the atmosphere pressing down against the surface, this poisonous stew of heated gases would discourage life as we know or can even imagine it.

Mariner 2's microwave at last gave us our first close "glimpse" beneath the surface of the clouds. Mariner 2 also made other calculations—sensing temperatures in the unbroken cloud layer by infrared radiometry, and calculating atmospheric density and composition. The pull Venus had on the Mariner spacecraft also made it possible to calculate the planet's mass with considerable accuracy. Exploration of Venus had begun—with just a little over half an hour of instrument scanning and data transmission.

Its job completed, Mariner 2 sped on into orbit around the Sun between Earth and Venus, where the first envoy to Venus now spins forever silent between the two worlds.

Early Soviet Probes and Venera 4
In planning planetary missions, timing is important—with everything primed for what is known as a "launch opportunity" or "window." As the target planet and Earth each travels its own elliptical orbit around the Sun, the point where the two are posi-

The Greenhouse Effect

A victim of the so-called "greenhouse effect," Venus's fiery atmosphere is the result of its close proximity to the Sun and its inability to partially disperse its tremendous "heat load" back out into space.

All planets absorb energy from the Sun in the form of shortwave solar radiation. This energy (which we call sunlight) is then reradiated outward as longer wave infrared radiation. The surface temperature of a planet is determined by the balance between the sunlight it absorbs and the infrared energy it emits. The temperature rises if a planet absorbs much more radiation than it gives off.

On Venus the cooling process is particularly hindered by the thick Venusian atmosphere, which acts something like a one-way gate, permitting the shortwave solar radiation to enter, but inhibiting or preventing the longer wavelength infrared radiation from escaping—trapping the emitted energy like the lid on a pot and causing the planet to heat up.

Many scientists fear that an increase of carbon dioxide in the Earth's atmosphere, caused by continual burning of fuels like gasoline and diesel, may also result in a greenhouse effect and that a gradual accumulation of trapped "heat" may eventually make the Earth too hot for human survival.

Although this effect is often called the "greenhouse effect" or sometimes a "runaway greenhouse effect," the terms are a little misleading since the common backyard greenhouse operates not just by trapping solar radiation, but also by preventing effective convection and mixing of the cool air outside the greenhouse and the warmer air inside.

---

tioned for the most oblique approach provides the best opportunity for getting there with the least fuel.

These opportunities don't happen often—in fact, for Venus they occur only once every 18 months. So, after the failure of Venera 1 in 1961, the Soviets geared up for three different launches in late August and early September 1962 (probably to take advantage of the same "window" that the U.S. Mariner 2 had taken off into). The Soviets usually tried to send a pair of spacecraft to Venus at the same time—a policy that would pay off in the future—making it possible to compare data from two simultaneous missions. Although we're not sure, it seems likely that the spacecraft launched on August 25, September 1 and September 12 were headed toward Venus. In a disappointing sequence, all three went no further than Earth orbit and finally burned up in the Earth's atmosphere.

During 1963, the Soviets continued testing their instruments, and on April 2, 1964, they launched

Zond 1, but the probe lost contact with Earth a month later and was finally pulled into solar orbit by the Sun's gravity. Back-to-back Venera 2 and 3 spacecraft, launched in November 1965, both lost contact with Earth before they arrived at Venus. But, with scientists tracking by radar, Venera 3 did actually impact the planet—becoming the first spacecraft ever to land on another planet. A third November try, Cosmos 96, remained caught in Earth orbit and burned up about two weeks after launch.

With Venera 4, the Soviets met with real success, moving exploration of Venus into an exciting new phase—the atmospheric entry probe. Launched on June 12, 1967, Venera 4 flew solo; its probable companion craft, Cosmos 167, was launched five days later, but never left Earth orbit.

October 18 saw Venera 4's arrival as it flew by Venus, collecting readings on the upper atmosphere and solar wind. As it passed, it released an 846-pound (384-kg) capsule to plummet down through the

Venusian atmosphere. For 94 exciting minutes of descent by parachute, the capsule's instruments transmitted the first on-site data on the atmosphere of Venus. For altitudes from 34 to 16 miles (55 to 25 km) it sent back readings for atmospheric temperature, pressure, density, wind velocity, and chemical composition before falling silent. Based on the Venera 4 experience, the Soviets would redesign future spacecraft for longer survival in the hostile Venusian environment.

Mariner 5

Meanwhile, the United States also had its eyes on the same launch opportunity the Soviets had used for Venera 4. So, on June 14, 1967, with its four solar panels reversed away from the Sun and a heat shield added, Mariner 5 was launched. Just one day after the Soviet probe, it arrived carrying an ultraviolet photometer and telemetry equipment, but unlike a previous Mariner mission to Mars, no TV camera.

In general, this flyby mission was similar to Mariner 2's, with a few improvements. On arrival it began transmitting information about the planet from a distance of 2,480 miles (3,991 km). This mission found the same high temperatures on the night side of the planet as had already been discovered on the sunlit side. Unlike the Moon, with its extreme night/day temperature differences, scientists concluded, Venus held its temperature constant with its dense atmospheric blanket and the rapid circulation of heated gases by constant winds.

Meanwhile, other breakthroughs in our study of Venus came from ground-based efforts, at the Deep Space Network in Goldstone, California, and the radio telescope at Arecibo, Puerto Rico. Venus, it turned out, rotates on its axis only once every 243 Earth days—a fact that had almost completely eluded scientists because the clouds, propelled by very rapid winds, spin so rapidly around the surface they hide. At the same time astronomers confirmed that an astronaut standing on the Venusian surface would see sunrise in the west—because Venus moves east to west on its axis, in a retrograde rotation. The cause of this curiosity (shared only with Uranus among the planets) still remains a mystery.

Strangely enough, it takes Venus longer to rotate on its axis (243 Earth days) than it does to travel around the Sun—a path the planet completes in the equivalent of 225 Earth days. As a result, the day/night cycle is influenced both by the planet's orbit around the Sun and its rotation, producing a daylight period of 58.5 days.

Venera 5-8

Although the Soviets did some scientific apparatus tests in the meantime, their Venus exploration program really took off in 1969. They launched a series of three probes—Venera 5, 6 and 7, the first two in January 1969 and the last in August 1970—to explore the chemical composition, pressure, density and temperature of the atmosphere at various locations on the Venusian globe.

The twin landers Venera 5 and 6 parachuted into the atmosphere a day apart, May 16 and 17, but they didn't make it to the surface. Both lasted under an hour, traveling between 22.37 to 23.6 miles (36 to 38 km) into the atmosphere and transmitting some data before being crushed by the pressure, but they prepared the way for the next Soviet foray, Venera 7.

On December 15, 1970, the Venera 7 descent craft headed for the surface, braking dramatically from 25,500 mph (41,400 kph) to 450 mph (724 kph) and enduring the incredible pressure and heat caused by the force of the descent. Its parachute, designed to withstand temperatures up to 986 degrees F (530 degrees C), ballooned above it, while the craft reported gradually increasing temperatures. For 23 minutes Venera 7 sent back the first transmission ever made from another planet's surface.

Sixteen months later, with a March 27, 1972 launch, the Soviets headed for yet another success with a similar probe, Venera 8. Once again, the probe transmitted from the atmosphere as it braked toward the planet surface on July 22. But this time, the probe lasted longer on the surface, recording a 752 degrees F (400 degrees C) temperature and sending back data for an impressive 50 minutes. It measured atmospheric pressure and wind velocity, and gave us first-hand knowledge about the composition of Venusian soil—indicating the presence of uranium, potassium and thorium in amounts similar to some rock formations found on Earth.

Mariner 10

With Mariner 10 we at last got a camera-eye view of the Venusian clouds from orbit. Launched November 3, 1973, this spacecraft was the result of more than a decade of evolution of the Mariner technology. It was designed to fly by Mercury as well, and its two-planet slingshot trajectory was the triumph of at least 20 years of speculation and engineering breakthroughs. Carrying two telescopic cameras, magnetometers, an ultraviolet (UV) spectrometer and a charged particle detector, on its way to Mercury Mariner 10 looked in

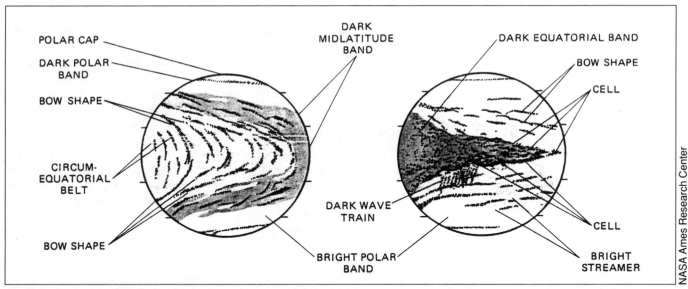

Venusian cloud features as seen in ultraviolet images taken by *Pioneer Venus*. These two views typically alternate every two days

on Venus. On February 5, 1974, the veiled planet loomed only 3,595 miles (5,784 km) away.

The results were spectacular—more than 3,500 TV pictures provided an array of stunning close-ups of the swirling mass of clouds that bounces sunlight so brilliantly into our morning and evening skies. Striking details of cloud circulation patterns around the equator and from the poles became visible for the first time in photos that provided 7,000 times the resolution we can obtain from Earth.

In addition, the UV filters made it possible to track the global circulation of the Venusian atmosphere. The data confirmed that the atmosphere of Venus whips around the planet in four days, while the ground beneath makes its incredibly slow 243-day rotation. At the edge of the disk we could also see the lower layers of clouds moving below the speeding upper cloud deck.

We gained many new clues about the history of our mysterious neighbor. The spectrometer picked up on the presence of large quantities of hydrogen, helium and atoms of oxygen in the high clouds of Venus—a strong indication that water vapor, now broken up into its components hydrogen and oxygen, was once present in quantity in the atmosphere.

All these clues were detected as Mariner 10 glided by, using the assistance of Venus's gravity to wing on toward Mercury.

Venera 9-10

Despite these successes, we still had never seen the surface of Venus close up—a problem the Soviet photographic landers Venera 9 and 10 were about to remedy in 1975.

Launched in June and arriving in October, Venera 9 and 10 were the first missions to Venus to combine a lander and an orbiter in one spacecraft. After arriving at Venus, each spacecraft separated into its component parts. The two landers then descended through the atmosphere to sites 1,240 miles (2,000 km) apart, each transmitting for an hour and sending back one exciting black-and-white photo apiece—the first—of the Venusian surface. Meanwhile, the two orbiters circled above.

Imagine what scientists might conclude about Earth's surface based on just two photos taken at surface level of, say, the base of the Adirondack Mountains in New York State and the Mojave Desert in California. It would be, at best, incomplete. Through the eyes of Venera 9 we surveyed a patch of stones and rocks such as we might expect to find on a hillside, while Venera 10 gave us a shot of a smoother surface—perhaps a geologically older plain or plateau. The two landers gave us just a glimpse—revealing basaltic-type rocks possibly formed by volcanic action and also reporting low, breeze-like wind velocities at the surface—but it was an exciting beginning.

Pioneer Venus

Up to 1978 humankind had scanned the clouds of Venus, sent probes plummeting into its atmospheric soup and, with Venera 7 to 10, landed probes on its

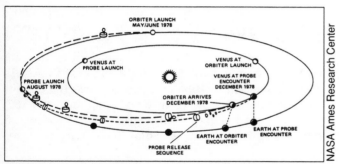

Pioneer Orbiter and Multiprobe launches and flight paths to Venus. Although the Multiprobe was launched two months later, it followed a shorter path and got to Venus just a few days after Orbiter.

surface. But we still did not have an overall picture of the planet.

Enter the Pioneer Venus mission developed at NASA Ames Research Center. Packing a lot of punch in a small space, Pioneer Venus was a back-to-back double launch of an orbiter and a multi-probe spacecraft.

The orbiter (sometimes called Pioneer 12), was launched May 20, 1978 and arrived at Venus on December 4. On board, most of the 12 experiments it performed explored aspects of the planet's atmosphere, but the real excitement was provided by the spacecraft's radar system, which mapped a whopping 90% or more of Venus's surface as it orbited.

In the images sent back by Pioneer we could now distinctly see objects as small as 60 miles (100 km) across, and together they provided scientists with the first global map of the Venusian terrain. They could distinguish continent-like highlands, hill plains, large, volcano-like mountains, and flat lowlands. Only fairly large-scale features showed up, of course, but at last we had an overall view of the surface—a major breakthrough.

For the most part, we discovered, the surface of Venus appears to be flat and barren, with large expanses of rolling plains, marked occasionally by craters and a few isolated mountains that jut up like islands in the overall evenness. Two massive high plateau areas—Aphrodite Terra near Venus's equator and Ishtar Terra to the north—resemble the continents of Earth. In a third major region, Beta Regio, two huge, possibly active, volcanoes appear to dominate the terrain. Water surrounding these areas, if there ever was any, has long since evaporated. In Ishtar Terra the peaks of Maxwell Montes—possibly an active volcano site—tower higher than Mt. Everest,

forming one of the highest mountains in the Solar System.

Large trench-like scars crisscrossing the crust in eastern Aphrodite Terra may be rift valleys possibly indicating that plate tectonics (the folding and faulting of large areas) are at work sculpturing the Venusian surface.

The second Pioneer Venus (sometimes known as Pioneer 13), was launched August 8 the same year and arrived in orbit just five days after Pioneer Venus 1 (Pioneer 12). Four capsules—one large and three small—peeled off on widely separated paths from the Pioneer 13 "bus" or carrier and plunged into the atmosphere, measuring, testing and transmitting data back to Earth as they went.

The probes had four main missions: first, to study the composition and nature of the clouds by taking measurements and samples, second, to study the Venusian atmosphere's composition and structure all the way from high altitudes to the surface, third, to investigate the atmosphere's circulation around the planet and, fourth, to find out how the atmosphere interacts with light and heat.

Highlights included a readout at 43.5 miles (70 km) indicating a powerful increase in sulfur dioxide. This led to intense speculation about the level of volcanic activity on the Venusian surface—possibly as much as 10 times that of all eruptions on Earth. This is still the subject of considerable debate among planetary experts.

In addition, Pioneer Venus probes found traces of noble or inert, gases in concentrations differing from those found on Mars and Earth. Noble gases interest

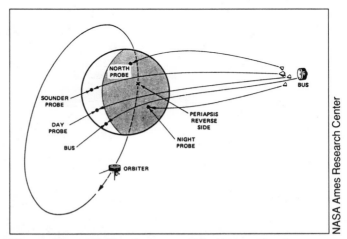

Pioneer Venus Multiprobe approach to Venus, showing release of the four probes from the bus and the five landing sites on the surface. Meanwhile, the Orbiter circled above the planet.

planetary scientists because they don't interact with other substances—remaining pure from the beginning of time. So the differences observed by Pioneer indicate that from the beginning Venus's make-up was probably unlike Earth's and Mars's. These findings also were at odds with some theories of planetary evolution.

Pioneer Venus probes found large amounts of deuterium (heavy hydrogen), in quantities more than 100 times those found on Earth, pointing again to a time when Venus may have had oceans. And Pioneer Venus further confirmed other measurements—including extremely high temperatures at the surface, the composition of Venus's lower atmosphere and the responsibility of the greenhouse effect for the high, infernal temperatures.

The four messengers and their bus were burned as a result of their efforts, but the data they obtained

continues to supply a wealth of information about the mystery planet—providing the first really extensive look at the "air" of another planet.

Meanwhile, hardy Pioneer 12 continues to orbit and send us news from above the skies of Venus. In 1984, and again in 1986 and 1987, as visiting comets came streaming around the Sun, operators at NASA Ames succeeded in repointing the stalwart spacecraft to investigate still another Solar System mystery (see Chapter 10).

In spring 1992, if all goes well, Pioneer 12 will move into the third phase of its mission—one last radar pass at the planet, covering areas it couldn't reach during its 1978 radar mapping phase. It will also take new measurements in the southern ionosphere and then finally plunge into the atmosphere, ending its triumphal 14-year jaunt—the longest ever aimed at a single planet.

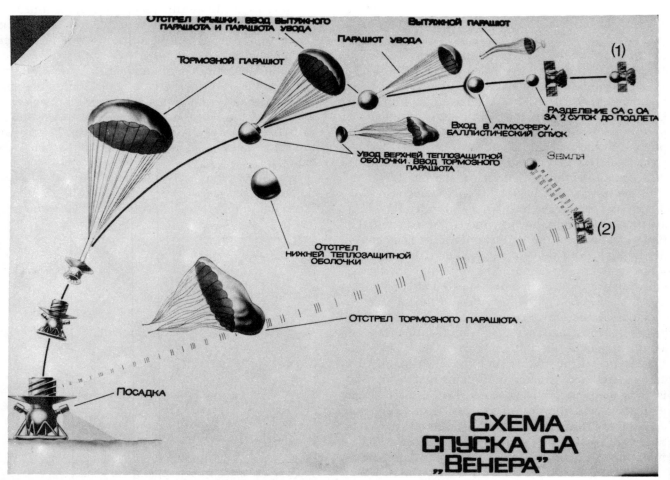

Venera 13 landing, showing separation of the probe from the orbiter (1) at upper right, deployment of the parachute to slow descent, then separation of the probe from the parachute followed by the probe's landing (left). Once landed, the probe transmits signals (seen here as broken lines) to the orbiter (2).

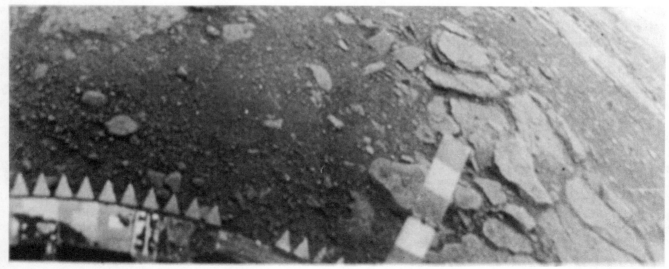

The surface of Venus as viewed by Venera 13

Venera 11-16

Following closely on the launch of NASA's Pioneer Venus mission, the Soviets sent out Venera 11 and 12 in September 1978—both also arriving at Venus, like the Pioneers, in December of that year. Each was made up of two modules, an orbiter and a lander, and gathered evidence of thunder and lightning in the atmosphere and measured traces of noble gases (including krypton, which was not detected by Pioneer Venus). Confusingly, the concentrations of noble gases, unlike those found by Pioneer Venus, were *similar* to those found on the Earth and Mars—adding yet another mystery to our neighbor's past.

Continuing their systematic exploration, the Soviets made two more tandem spaceflights to Venus at the next opportunity, in late October and early November 1981. This time, with two orbiter-lander combinations, the Soviets would take us back for another exciting look at the surface of Venus. Venera 13 and 14 both arrived in March 1982, making their way through the thick, corrosive atmosphere, and landing safely. From there they sent back the first color photos of the Venusian surface.

For the first time we viewed the peachy to bright orange hue of the Venusian sky. Through Venera 13, landing southeast of Phoebe Regio, we seemed to be looking at a plain strewn with rocks, eroded perhaps by the caustic atmosphere, and dotted with rocky outcrops amidst areas of fine-grained material. Soil analysis tests run by Venera 13 revealed the same kind of rocks as those found by Venera 8, basaltic with a high potassium content—rare on Earth, but found

in regions where continents are being pulled apart, such as East African rift valleys and the Rio Grande rift valleys in North America.

From its site 590 miles (950 km) to the southeast, however, Venera 14 focused on a different setting

Model of the Venera 15 spacecraft

with less fine-grained material but more layered rocks and small potholes varying in color. Here the soil analysis showed lava-like basalts more similar to those found on Earth's ocean floors.

Moving back to the overview, in June 1983 the Soviets sent Venera 15 and 16 to map Venus at a resolution of about 1.2 miles (2 km)—giving us bird's-eye radar glimpses at much closer range than Pioneer Venus. With the corroboration of the Arecibo radio telescope in Puerto Rico, this close view for the first time revealed the sure presence of impact craters on the surface of Venus. Although they were able to cover only about 30% of the planet, the regions near its north pole, Venera 15 and 16 provided a valuable complement to Pioneer Venus.

VEGA 1 and 2

Zooming toward a March 1986 appointment with Comet Halley (see Chapter 10), the Soviets' twin spacecraft VEGA 1 and VEGA 2 did double duty. They dropped identical two-part probes into the atmospheric soup of Venus—in what turned out to be another ambitious planetary mission, bringing to 19 the number of Soviet probes launched to Venus in 23 years, involving participation by a total of nine countries (including three western European). And, in an unusual move by both the USSR and the United States, a handful of American investigators also took part in the VEGA missions.

Launched in December 1984 at Tyuratam on the steppes of central Asia, VEGA 1 and VEGA 2 carried aboard identical probes and approached the planet on the night side. VEGA 1 arrived the night of June 10-11, aimed toward Aphrodite Terra, with its partner angling in four nights later about 1,000 miles south and a little east. This time, unfortunately, the lack of light would prevent the spectacular surface photography of Venera 13 and 14.

Each probe was composed of two separate parts—a descent probe/surface lander and an atmospheric balloon—each with a separate program of experiments.

The 10-foot-diameter balloons each dangled a 5-foot package of atmospheric instruments at the end of a 40-foot tether as they drifted through the Venusian atmosphere at an altitude of 34 miles, collecting data about the dense cloud layers as they went. Wind velocities discovered by the VEGA balloons turned out to be much higher than the experiment designers had expected—150 mph (240 kph) as opposed to an expected 20-30 mph (32-48 kph). Additionally, they found far more turbulence than expected at that altitude.

The VEGA balloons also measured temperatures within the cloud layer, vertical wind (movement of gases between the surface and upper atmosphere) and atmospheric pressure. In addition, they looked at chemical composition (especially water vapor and sulfur dioxide concentration), atmospheric density and the location of clouds. Together the two balloons sent back more than 90 hours of useful data to a worldwide international tracking operation that included NASA's Deep Space Network.

Meanwhile, the VEGA landers made the first nighttime landing in the history of Venusian exploration. On the way down they deployed parachutes and began taking data from an altitude of 16 miles, for the first time collecting information about trace elements in the lower atmosphere.

VEGA 1 soft-landed on the surface in a low-plain area just north of Aphrodite—a type of terrain never before explored. Unfortunately, on the way down, the soil sampler went awry and began "taking samples" 10 miles above the surface. However, the rest of the experiments went well, with 20 minutes of data transmission, and new information was picked up about an area not mapped by either Venera 15-16 or by Earth-based radar.

Aboard VEGA 2, the scooper worked fine, and 36 minutes of data came through about the plain area on which the probe had landed. It was an area well explored by Pioneer Venus mapping, which pleased scientists who hoped to compare the remote sensing data from Pioneer with the VEGA surface sampling for new insights into the geochemistry of the area and its lower atmosphere.

Questions Still Unanswered

Many questions still remain about the veiled planet. Is Venus "alive" with volcanic activity, or is it a "dead" planet, pock-marked with impact craters? Is the atmosphere charged with lightning hovering over active volcanic regions? What erosive forces have affected the planet's surface in the past—such as winds or water flow? Did oceans once spread across its surface?

Why did our nearest neighbor, so similar in size and density, evolve so differently from Earth? Is its carbon dioxide atmosphere and hot, searing surface a portent of our own future? Why does Venus have no intrinsic magnetic field? Why does it have no satellites? Why does Venus rotate "backwards," with the Sun rising in the west? And why does its atmosphere spin so much more rapidly than the slowly rotating planet? The mysteries remain unsolved.

Future Mission Plans

Magellan

Some of those mysteries may at last be unshrouded by Magellan, a small, compact craft launched from the U.S. Space Shuttle Atlantis in April 1989. Simple and economical in design, the 2,150-pound (975-kg) spacecraft houses only one instrument— a Synthetic Aperture Radar (SAR) system. With it, scientists hope to answer some final questions about the veiled planet's compelling topography. One of the more controversial questions likely to be answered by Magellan is whether Venus is "alive" with active volcanism as many scientists suspect.

Clearly, as shown by Pioneer 12 and Venera 15-16, radar imaging is the way to "see" through the dense Venusian clouds. But past imaging missions have either lacked resolution in favor of breadth of coverage (Pioneer) or have covered only small areas in favor of higher resolution (Venera 15-16 missions).

Thorough coverage *and* high-resolution imaging, though, are Magellan's strengths. With its large, 12-foot (3.7-meter) antenna dish and a resolution 100 times that delivered by Pioneer Venus, and about 10 times greater than any mission since, the system should reveal features as small as 820 feet (250 m) across in swaths covering 70% or more of the planet's surface. The result will be an extraordinary quantity of data. Calculated in terms of picture elements, or pixels, Magellan will send back to Earth about as much image data as have all U.S. planetary missions—to any planet—to date.

Magellan project chief John H. Gerpheide expects the radar imaging to answer a lot of questions—making it possible to distinguish between cratering and volcanism, to see the tectonics, to observe any erosive mechanisms there may be, like winds and water, and to detect remnants of ocean basins if they exist. It will also chart global topography—the height of the Venusian terrain—which, together with the images, will provide insights into the geological history of Venus. Magellan will also provide data that will help scientists develop a better idea of what's going on in the interior of Venus.

Vesta

Soviet scientists, too, have talked tentatively about at least one more look at Venus, although Vesta, as the mission is called, may not get off the ground without the help of a European partner. One plan calls for this multiple-asteroid encounter to focus on the asteroid Vesta, dropping off a lander—probably in the northern part of the Venusian "continent" of Ishtar—as the spacecraft zooms by Venus for a gravity assist.

Both the United States and the USSR are now turning most of their planetary explorations toward Mars, but the Mariners, Veneras, Pioneers, VEGAs—and even Magellan and Vesta—still will not have answered all our questions about our elusive neighbor, Venus.

3

THE MOON: OUR NEAREST NEIGHBOR IN SPACE

It is a most beautiful and delightful sight . . .
—Galileo Galilei, after viewing the Moon
through his new telescope

This has been far more than three men on a mission to the Moon; more still than the efforts of a government and industry team; more even than the efforts of one nation. We feel that this stands as a symbol of the insatiable curiosity of all mankind to explore the unknown.
—Edwin Aldrin, during a broadcast
from *Apollo 11* from space

Locked together in a close cosmic dance, Earth and Moon, planet and satellite, revolve around their common center of gravity. The larger one, green-blue-white, bursting with color, water and life. The other, smaller by nearly three-quarters, colorless, scarred, cratered and marked by time. Its hidden face, dark and pitted, is turned perpetually toward the stars. What tragedy occurred in the long-distant past to leave the Moon so cold and desolate?

At once our most familiar and most mysterious neighbor in space, the Moon has intrigued the human mind since the first pair of human eyes turned upward toward the sky and wondered. From ancient mythologies to modern popular songs, people have invented many faces for the Moon, most of them kind. The Egyptians associated the God Thoth, patron of arts and learning, with the Moon, and for the Babylonians the Moon god, Sin, was the source of the calendar and wisdom. Greeks and Romans both had

their Moon goddesses. In popular culture lovers sang songs about it, under it, and to it; ambitious scientists shot rockets at it; and, according to many low-budget horror movies, it turned nice, quiet young men into howling, vicious werewolves.

For the more serious-minded, though, the Moon was no less fascinating. The regularity of the Moon's motion across the sky and its changing phases helped human observers to keep watch over time and seasons, and the Moon was one of the first celestial objects Galileo explored with his telescope in 1610. Since ancient times humans have known that our pale yellow companion in the sky is related to the ocean tides, and Isaac Newton's explanation that the tides occur because of the Moon's gravitational attraction added explanation to observation.

A scant (by cosmic standards) mean distance of 238,855 miles (384,390 km) away from the Earth, with an equatorial diameter of 2,160 miles (3,476 km), the

The Earth's Moon

Position: Satellite of Earth
Average Distance from Sun: 238,855 miles (384,390 km)
Diameter: 2,160 miles (3,476 km), 27.3% the size of Earth
Mass: 0.0123 times Earth's
Density: 3.34 (Water = 1)
Volume: 0.0203 times Earth's
Surface Gravity: 0.165 times Earth's
Period of Rotation on Axis: Once every 27.322 Earth days
Revolution around Earth: Once every 27.322 Earth days (sidereal period);
  29.53-day revolution as seen from Earth
Orbital Speed: 0.63 miles/sec (1.02 km/sec)

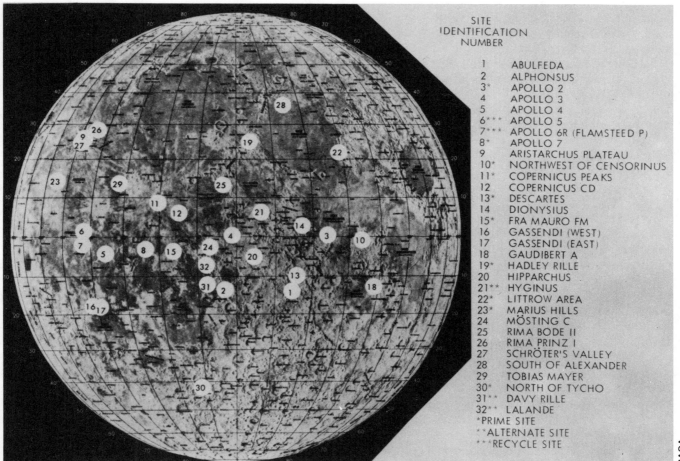

SITE IDENTIFICATION NUMBER

1 ABULFEDA
2 ALPHONSUS
3* APOLLO 2
4 APOLLO 3
5 APOLLO 4
6*** APOLLO 5
7*** APOLLO 6R (FLAMSTEED P)
8* APOLLO 7
9 ARISTARCHUS PLATEAU
10* NORTHWEST OF CENSORINUS
11* COPERNICUS PEAKS
12 COPERNICUS CD
13* DESCARTES
14 DIONYSIUS
15* FRA MAURO FM
16 GASSENDI (WEST)
17 GASSENDI (EAST)
18 GAUDIBERT A
19* HADLEY RILLE
20 HIPPARCHUS
21** HYGINUS
22* LITTROW AREA
23* MARIUS HILLS
24 MÖSTING C
25 RIMA BODE II
26 RIMA PRINZ I
27 SCHRÖTER'S VALLEY
28 SOUTH OF ALEXANDER
29 TOBIAS MAYER
30* NORTH OF TYCHO
31** DAVY RILLE
32** LALANDE
*PRIME SITE
**ALTERNATE SITE
***RECYCLE SITE

NASA

This map of the Moon shows the location of landing sites considered for the U.S. manned missions known as the **Apollo program**

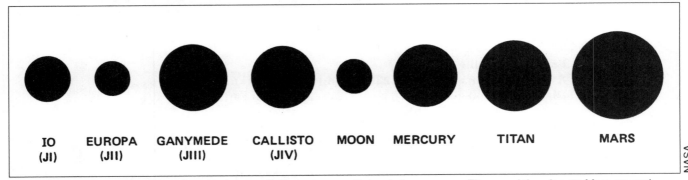

IO (JI) EUROPA (JII) GANYMEDE (JIII) CALLISTO (JIV) MOON MERCURY TITAN MARS

NASA

Earth's Moon compared with Jupiter's four large Galilean moons, Saturn's large moon, Titan, and the planets Mercury and Mars

Moon reveals striking features even to a relatively weak telescope such as you might use in your backyard. Large, dark, apparently smooth plains can be seen, as well as brighter areas spotted with mountains and craters. An alien world illuminated against the darkness around it, it is at once comforting and disquieting. Where did it come from, this place so close that it appears to look back at us across a narrow passage of darkness? What is it like, this world that seems so silent, so motionless? Why is it here, such a striking presence against the dark of night?

Although the scientific study of the Moon has occupied humanity for thousands of years, it wasn't until the arrival of the space age that we began to find answers to some of its mysteries. Like the telescope, and the camera before it, the rocket gave humanity a new tool that could help unravel the Moon's many secrets.

The Space-Age Moon

July 20, 1969 brought the Moon home to many people. As Neil Armstrong and Buzz Aldrin took their first cautious steps on the Moon's surface, Michael Collins orbited overhead in the command module of Apollo 11, a tiny spacecraft destined to become one of the most famous machines in humankind's history. After centuries of observation, study and theory, humanity walked on the Moon, and studied firsthand its alien wonder. It was, as reported from the Moon's surface by Armstrong, "one small step for man . . . one giant leap for mankind." But Apollo 11 was only one in a long line of Moon-targeted spacecraft that began only a few years after the space age opened with the Earth-orbiting flight of the Soviet satellite dubbed Sputnik on October 4, 1957.

Beginning with the unsuccessful Thor-Able 1, August 17, 1958, and stretching to the present, the U.S. and Soviet space programs have launched over 80 spacecraft toward the Moon. Of those, around 40 have been successful and returned data back to Earth. While it is generally believed that the U.S. and Soviets "raced to the Moon," in a competition ending with the successful manned U.S. Apollo missions, observers note that differences in the programs may make the idea of such a "race" unfounded. Both began with simple and often unsuccessful spacecraft and gradually developed heavier boosters and more sophisticated payloads. Under President John Kennedy's administration, the U.S. emphasized manned lunar landings while the Soviets moved toward more complex automated spacecraft.

Starting with its basic and limited Pioneer spacecraft and moving into the slightly more advanced Ranger series, the U.S. experienced more than a half-dozen failures before achieving its first limited success in April 1962, when the spacecraft Ranger 4 crash-landed on the Moon's far side—the first U.S. probe to hit the Moon. After two more disappointments the slightly modified Ranger 7 became America's first lunar success. Launched on July 28, 1964, it took and returned over 4,300 close-up high-resolution pictures of the Moon's surface before destroying itself on impact. The Soviet Luna series, meanwhile, had actually scored the first crash-landing on the Moon with Luna 2, launched on September 12, 1959, and the first lunar photos were taken by Luna 3, launched on October 4, 1959. Although Luna 3's photos were fuzzy, they did allow the Soviets to produce the first rough map ever made of the Moon's far side (which never turns toward Earth and had never been viewed before).

With Rangers 8 and 9 in February and March of 1965 the United States succeeded in returning over 12,000 more high-resolution photographs of the lunar surface, including close-ups of the dark, flat "plains" called maria (plural of Latin *mare*, meaning "sea" although, of course, there is no water). These par-

Ranger 9 view of Alphonsus Crater on the Moon

NASA Jet Propulsion Laboratory

ticular photos were what U.S. scientists had been waiting for. The maria were primarily smooth, craterless and featureless, hiding a few deep crevasses or dangerously large boulders. In short, good landing sites for America's first attempt to make an unmanned soft-landing on the Moon's surface.

Once again, though, the Soviets, too, were on the mark. After five unsuccessful tries at placing a soft-landed and safely operating spacecraft on the Moon in 1965 (Luna 5 struck the Moon but did not succeed

in soft-landing), Luna 9 landed perfectly in January 1966, sending back medium-grade pictures from the surface for four days before finally running out of power. In May 1966, America's Surveyor 1 soft-landed successfully near the Flamsteed Crater, taking over a thousand photos and returning data on the lunar soil consistency. The Soviet Luna 13, launched December 21, 1966, on the heels of a couple of Soviet lunar orbiters, gave the Soviets their second soft-landing, more photos, and samples for soil analysis. The Ranger, Luna and Surveyor series proved we could get to the Moon and opened up the lunar surface for scientific investigation. The era of lunar exploration had opened. It was an era that would boom with all the excitement of the American Gold Rush over the next few years. A thousand scientific instruments on both Earth and lunar surfaces were unlocking more secrets of the planets and universe each day.

With the Apollo program, from its first manned lunar landing in July 1969 until its last, Apollo 17 in December 1972, the United States put a total of 12 men carrying scientific instruments on the surface of the Moon. Veering away from what may or may not have been a planned program of manned lunar landings, the Soviets successfully launched more orbiters and also landed two brilliantly conceived lunar

NASA Johnson Space Center

Harrison Schmitt scoops up samples from the Moon's surface during the Apollo 17 mission

Making Contact with the Moon:
U.S. and Soviet Missions Since 1958

	Mission		Launch Date
1958	Pioneer 0	U.S.	August 17
	Pioneer 1	U.S.	October 11
	Pioneer 2	U.S.	November 8
	Pioneer 3	U.S.	December 6
1959	Luna 1	USSR	January 2
	Pioneer 4	U.S.	March 3
	*Luna 2	USSR	September 12
	Pioneer (P1)	U.S.	September 24
	*Luna 3	USSR	October 4
	Pioneer (P30)	U.S.	November 26
1960	Pioneer (P30)	U.S.	September 25
	Pioneer (P31)	U.S.	December 15
1961	Ranger 1	U.S.	August 23
	Ranger 2	U.S.	November 18
1962	Ranger 3	U.S.	January 26
	Ranger 4	U.S.	April 23
	Ranger 5	U.S.	October 18
1963	Luna 4	USSR	April 2
1964	Ranger 6	U.S.	January 30
	*Ranger 7	U.S.	July 28
1965	*Ranger 8	U.S.	February 17
	Cosmos 60	USSR	March 12
	*Ranger 9	U.S.	March 21
	*Luna 5	USSR	May 9
	Luna 6	USSR	June 8
	*Zond 3	USSR	July 18
	Luna 7	USSR	October 4
	Luna 8	USSR	December 3
1966	*Luna 9	USSR	January 31
	Cosmos 111	USSR	March 1
	*Luna 10	USSR	March 31
	*Surveyor 1	U.S.	May 31
	Explorer 33	U.S.	July 1
	*Lunar Orbiter 1	U.S.	August 10
	*Luna 11	USSR	August 24
	Surveyor 2	U.S.	September 20
	*Luna 12	USSR	October 22
	*Lunar Orbiter 2	U.S.	November 6
	*Luna 13	USSR	December 21
1967	*Lunar Orbiter 3	U.S.	February 5
	*Surveyor 3	U.S.	April 17
	*Lunar Orbiter 4	U.S.	May 3
	Surveyor 4	U.S.	July 14
	*Explorer 35	U.S.	July 19
	*Lunar Orbiter 5	U.S.	August 1
	*Surveyor 5	U.S.	September 8

	*Surveyor 6	U.S.	November 7
1968	*Surveyor 7	U.S.	January 7
	*Zond 4	USSR	March 2
	*Luna 14	USSR	April 7
	*Zond 5	USSR	September 14
	*Apollo 7	U.S.	October 11
	*Zond 6	USSR	November 10
	*Apollo 8	U.S.	December 21
1969	*Apollo 9	U.S.	March 3
	*Apollo 10	U.S.	May 18
	Luna 15	USSR	July 13
	*Apollo 11	U.S.	July 16
	*Zond 7	USSR	August 7
	Cosmos 300	USSR	September 23
	Cosmos 305	USSR	October 22
	*Apollo 12	U.S.	November 14
1970	Apollo 13	U.S.	April 11
	*Luna 16	USSR	September 12
	*Zond 8	USSR	October 20
	*Luna 17/ Lunokhod 1	USSR	November 10
1971	*Apollo 14	U.S.	January 31
	*Apollo 15	U.S.	July 26
	*Apollo 15/ subsatellite	U.S.	August 4
	Luna 18	USSR	September 2
	*Luna 19	USSR	September 28
1972	*Luna 20	USSR	February 14
	*Apollo 16	U.S.	April 16
	*Apollo 16/ subsatellite	U.S.	April 24
	*Apollo 17	U.S.	December 7
1973	*Luna 21/ Lunokhod 2	USSR	January 8
	*Explorer 49	U.S.	June 10
1974	*Luna 22	USSR	May 29
	Luna 23	USSR	October 28
1976	*Luna 24	USSR	August 9
1990	Luna 25	USSR	(planned)
1993	Lunar geos- cience orbiter	U.S.	(planned)

Note: Launch dates for U.S. missions given are Greenwich Mean Time.

* Indicates a successful mission

robot/roving science laboratories—Lunokhod 1, in November 1970, and Lunokhod 2, in January 1973. Then, almost as suddenly as it had started, the lunar era was over, sputtering out as its last mission, Luna 24, sampled lunar soil in August 1976.

The Apollo Spacecraft

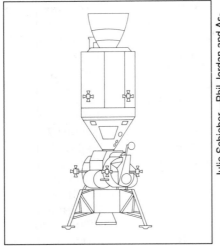

Julie Schieber—Phil Jordan and Associates Inc., © 1987, Phil Jordan and Associates

The Apollo spacecraft: command/service module (CSM) and lunar module (LM)

The first spacecraft to carry humans to another body in the Solar System, the Apollo spacecraft was an 82-foot vehicle launched atop a Saturn rocket.

Costing a total of $25 billion, the Apollo Project in all of its stages was humankind's most ambitious "space program." Although much of the Apollo project was political and sociological in nature, scientific experiments performed by the Apollo crews contributed greatly to the sum of knowledge about our nearest space neighbor.

The Apollo spacecraft was actually a composite of five parts—a command module (CM), service module (SM), lunar landing module (LM), launch escape system (LES) and spacecraft lunar adapter (SLA). Only the first three parts escaped Earth's gravity, the latter two being jettisoned early in the launch.

The nerve center of the spacecraft, the command module, was the actual working and living quarters for Apollo's three-person crew during its journey to the Moon. The CM was also the only part of the spacecraft to return to Earth.

The SM, largest of the modules, held the electrical power subsystem, environmental control subsystem and propulsion subsystems. It was jettisoned on the return journey just before the spacecraft entered Earth's atmosphere.

The only part of the spacecraft to touch down on the Moon, the lunar module, was itself actually two parts: (1) a descent module to carry its two-person crew to the lunar surface and (2) an ascent module to return them to the orbiting command/service modules. The LM served as a lunar base while on the Moon, holding living quarters, life support systems, communications equipment and scientific equipment.

In later Apollo missions the LM also carried aboard the Lunar Roving Vehicle, used by the astronauts to drive over the Moon's surface.

Looking Back on the First Lunar Era

Perhaps the most important legacy of our lunar exploration was a greater understanding of the Moon, a greater appreciation for the Earth itself and a key to some of the mysteries of our Solar System. We have seen a world barren and desolate, too small and with too light a mass to hold on to an atmosphere. Unlike the Earth, the Moon is a world stunted and locked into its own past without growth or change—a world now so static that footprints left on its dusty surface may last a million years. It's a kind of fossil that tells the history of our Solar System and our own planet. Our journeys to the Moon have already taught us much about ourselves and the wondrous rarity of our own existence.

The Mystery of the Moon

Perhaps the biggest mystery remaining about the Moon is whether it is our natural "sister" or has been "adopted." Why does the Earth have a satellite so large in relation to its own size? And where did it come from? A look at how the Moon is like the Earth, and how it differs, may be the place to begin.

We know, from studies of data taken from orbit and lunar samples returned by exploring spacecraft, that the Moon is approximately the same age as the Earth—4.5 billion years old. Similarities in the relative abundance of oxygen isotopes in nearly identical proportions between the Earth and the Moon suggest that both bodies formed in the same region of the Solar System. The Moon has no atmosphere and no water or organic compounds (carbon-containing substances that can form living things). It also has smaller amounts of elements like sodium that evaporate easily and a much smaller iron core in relation to its mass. Unlike the Earth, the Moon is without magnetic poles and has only the most miniscule of magnetic fields, so tiny in fact as to be practically non-existent.

Visually the Earth and Moon are striking contrasts. While the Earth is green, verdant, and flowing with water, the dry, lifeless Moon is marked by rugged mountain ranges, large smooth areas and thousands of meteorite impact craters. The darkish flat areas, the maria, which take up about 15% of the Moon's surface, are believed to have been created by lava flows swelling out of the Moon's interior. Younger than the "highlands," the maria have many fewer impact craters, and are more prominent on the side of the Moon that faces the Earth, perhaps because of the Earth's gravitational pull. The far side of the Moon is more heavily cratered than the near side and is virtually without maria.

Up until recently most scientists have supported one of three main theories about the Moon's relationship with the Earth:

(1) The *fission* theory holds that the Moon was once a part of the primitive and molten Earth and was "spun off," like a blob of paint, by the Earth's rapid spin. The problem with this theory for most scientists, though, is that the Earth would have to have been spinning much faster than it is now to separate the Moon in this way. So fast in fact that an Earth day would have been only 2½ hours long!

(2) The *condensation* theory argues that the Moon was formed at the same time as the Earth, out of the same primitive materials that once formed a ring around the Earth, and then cohered into our familiar satellite. This "double-planet" theory has many supporters but also runs into trouble. It doesn't agree with mathematical calculations of the Earth's rotation rate and it also offers no explanation about why the material forming the Moon stayed in Earth orbit, instead of being drawn inward and becoming a part of the Earth itself.

(3) The *capture*, or "*adopted sister*," theory—one of the most colorful, if most unlikely—states that the Moon was formed complete somewhere else in the Solar System and then experienced some kind of catastrophe that knocked it toward the Earth, where it was captured by Earth's gravity to become a satellite. Although this scenario is remotely possible, it too is highly unlikely, calling for a once-in-a-lifetime billiard-ball shot that would put the Moon in just the right orbit around Earth rather than an entirely different orbit around the Sun. It also fails to account for the similarities in the the Earth's and Moon's composition.

Joining in the "big three" theories recently is a fourth—a kind of a hybrid that attempts to answer some of the problems in the others. To simplify this theory greatly, during the early days of the Earth's formation, while it was still molten and was slowly building up out of many smaller bodies called planetesimals, a large "left-over" planetesimal smashed into it. Part of both the Earth and the planetesimal vaporized and spewed the molten debris into orbit around the Earth, where it eventually became the Moon.

Which of these theories will turn out to be correct? Or does the answer lie in yet another theory? We don't know yet.

Humans on the Moon: The Apollo Missions

Mission	Astronauts	Dates
Apollo-Saturn 7	Schirra, Eisele, Cunningham	Oct. 11-22, 1968
	(Flight test in Earth Orbit)	
Apollo-Saturn 8	Borman, Lovell, Anders	Dec. 21-27, 1968
	(First humans in lunar orbit)	
Apollo-Saturn 9	McDivitt, Scott, Schweickart	March 3-13, 1969
	(Earth orbit test of lunar module)	
Apollo-Saturn 10	Stafford, Young, Cernan	May 18-26, 1969
	(Test for lunar landing)	
Apollo-Saturn 11	Armstrong, Collins, Aldrin	July 16-24, 1969
	(First human landing on Moon)	
Apollo-Saturn 12	Conrad, Gordon, Bean	Nov. 14-24, 1969
	(Second successful lunar crew)	
Apollo-Saturn 13	Lovell, Swigert, Haise	April 11-17, 1970
	(Mission aborted in space; safe return to Earth)	
Apollo-Saturn 14	Shepard, Roosa, Mitchell	Jan. 31-Feb. 9, 1971
	(Third successful lunar crew)	
Apollo-Saturn 15	Scott, Worden, Irwin	July 26-Aug. 7, 1971
	(Fourth successful lunar crew first use of lunar rover)	
Apollo-Saturn 16	Young, Mattingly, Duke	April 16-27, 1972
	(Fifth successful lunar crew)	
Apollo-Saturn 17	Cernan, Evans, Schmitt	Dec. 7-19, 1972
	(Sixth and last Apollo landing—first scientist (Schmitt) on Moon)	

The Known Territory of the Moon

Wherever and however the Moon originated, though, the U.S. and Soviet space missions have given scientists a fair idea of its geological history since that time.

Most scientists believe that at its formation the Moon was almost completely molten. As it began to cool, heavier material began to sink inward towards its core while the still molten surface was subjected to heavy meteorite bombardments—forming, obliterating, and reforming craters. Scientists believe that this major bombardment, which totally devastated the surface, stopped around 3.9 billion years ago.

Then, continuing its troubled progress to its present state, the Moon's interior began to melt again, heated by the decay of radioactive materials. From 4.2 to 3 billion years ago, rivers of molten lava ran across the surface, where they pooled in large lava "seas." These maria then cooled and froze, and at this stage the Moon "died"—its internal heat engine turned off and all large-scale geological activity ceased. Except for an occasional meteorite striking its surface and some-

30

times leaving its mark in the freshly formed *maria*, the Moon's face froze into the familiar surface we see today.

Whether this "history" provides a complete picture only further studies will tell. As with all objects in our solar system, the Moon still holds much to be learned. Even as we attempt to unravel its past, though, we are planning for its future.

The Moon in Our Future: The Return

No matter how dead the Moon's past, there can be little doubt that it will again see human life in the future. Strategically orbiting the Earth, our satellite represents a natural space base. Some have suggested we should mine the Moon for its valuable natural resources. Others call for military bases on the Moon for defense. We may want to use it as a jumping-off point for longer space expeditions, as some argue. And the quiet and advantageous view of its far side would provide an ideal setting for radio and optical astronomy. But, whatever our goals, in the future humankind will certainly be returning to the Moon, Earth's closest companion in the universe.

4

THE CHANGING FACES OF MARS

I believe that on the basis of the data we have on hand, we can't conclusively say that there is life on Mars . . . and we cannot conclusively say there is no life on Mars.
—Harold Klein, Mars Viking Science Team

Hey! Mars is a fun place!
—Michael H. Carr, Mars Viking Science Team

Under the pale pink sky only rocks litter the ground for miles. No movement, no bird, small animal or insect breaks across the silent gaze of the camera eye as it blinks its image hundreds of thousands of miles through silent space. Mechanically the eye shifts its gaze, again and again, looking, looking. From out of the sky it came, this metal ambassador, seeking answers to generations of questions, and one question above all others. Standing in the cold day of the alien world, its sensors begin slowly to work, gathering information, collecting data, relaying it back to its own home planet. And in the beam of messages sent slowly back, it begins the answer to the first question: Is there life?

Historical Mars

Of all the planets in our Solar System Mars has long been the favorite of science-fiction writers. It is the only body in the sky besides our own Moon to have surface features that can be seen through a telescope, and its reddish color suggests to the unaided human eye a world different from all the rest surrounding it in the sky.

Humankind's age-old infatuation with the red planet has been off-again and on-again. In our con-

stant fascination we have imagined it in a thousand different ways—from a planet like Earth, verdant and life-bearing, to an arid geological companion like the Moon. Always though, somewhere in the back of the human mind, has lingered the thought of life perhaps existing now or once long past on that distant planet. Science-fiction writers imagined strange creatures crawling across its surface. Sometimes these Martians were completely alien to the human eye, monsters drawn from our vivid imagination. Sometimes they took more human forms and even walked among us, bearing good or evil. But always they appeared alien and strange.

In the era before the space age, it was not just imaginative writers who saw Mars as a place teeming with life. Philosophers and scientists also were caught in the grip of that planet's fascinating spell. While most held out only a faint possibility of life existing in any form on the planet's alien surface, some, like the American astronomer Percival Lowell in 1894, imagined an intelligent life form on the planet so great that it carved out a vast network of artificially made canals to irrigate the planet's barren surface.

Mars: The Planet

Position: Fourth from Sun
Average Distance from Sun: 141.29 million miles (227.38 million km)—
   compared to Earth at 92.95 million miles (149.59 million km)
Diameter: 4,213 miles (6,780 km), 53% the size of Earth
Mass: 0.107 times Earth's
Density: 3.93 (Water = 1)
Volume: 0.15 times Earth's
Surface Gravity: 0.379 times Earth's
Period of Rotation on Axis: Once every 24.6 Earth hours
Revolution around Sun: Once every 686.98 Earth days (sidereal period)
Orbital Speed: 15.04 miles/sec (24.2 km/sec)
Satellites: Two

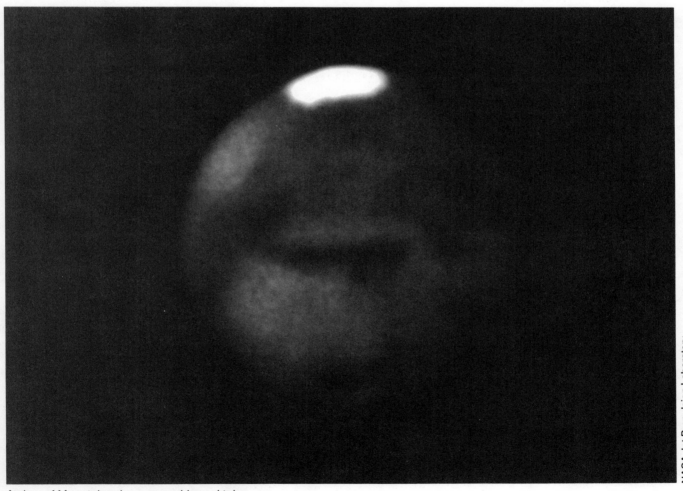

A view of Mars taken by a ground-based telescope

NASA Jet Propulsion Laboratory

Uncovering the Mysteries of Mars:
U.S. and Soviet Missions Since 1960

1960 **Mars-1960A, Mars-1960B** **USSR** Intended to fly as back-to-back flyby missions, these two spacecraft were launched October 10 and 14, but neither one ever reached Earth orbit.

1962 **Mars-1962A** **USSR** Launched October 24, this flyby mission failed before leaving Earth orbit.

Mars-1 **USSR** This flyby mission, launched November 1, started on its way but slipped out of contact on the way to Mars.

Mars-1962B **USSR** Launched November 4, this flyby mission also did not leave Earth orbit.

1964 **Mariner 3** **U.S.** Booster failure caused aborted mission for this flyby, launched November 5.

* Mariner 4 **U.S.** First successful mission to Mars, launched November 28, flew by and sent back the first close-up images.

Zond 2 **USSR** Intended to fly by and possibly land on Mars, launched November 30 and lost contact in flight.

1969 *** Mariner 6, Mariner 7** **U.S.** Successful back-to-back, photographic flyby missions, launched February 25 and March 25.

Mars-1969A, Mars-1969B **USSR** Launched March 27 and April 14, possibly intended to be lander missions, but failed to reach Earth orbit.

1971 **Mariner 8** **U.S.** Booster failure aborted this orbiter mission, launched May 8.

Cosmos 419 **USSR** An orbiter/lander mission that failed to leave Earth orbit when launched May 10.

Mars 2 **USSR** Launched on May 19, this orbiter/lander mission reached Mars with a successful orbiter phase, but the lander failed.

* Mars 3 **USSR** A second orbiter/lander mission, launched May 28. Again the orbiter worked well, but the lander failed after 110 seconds on the surface of Mars.

* Mariner 9 **U.S.** Launched May 30, this orbiter mission sent back the first photos of the Martian moons and mapped most of the surface of Mars.

1973 **Mars 4** **USSR** Launched July 21 and originally intended as an orbiter mission, became instead a flyby because of retrorocket failure.

*Mars 5 **USSR** Successful orbiter mission, launched July 25, gathered atmospheric data and took high-quality photos.

Mars 6 **USSR** A flyby/lander mission, launched August 5, which, after sending home some data, was lost from contact before landing occurred.

Mars 7 **USSR** Launched August 9, this flyby/lander mission failed when the lander missed the planet.

1975 ***Viking 1, Viking 2** **U.S.** August 20 and September 9 launches sent these back-to-back orbiter/lander missions to Mars where they completed the first two soft landings and sent back the first images and data from the surface of Mars.

1988 **Phobos** **USSR** Two spacecraft launched in July with three phases: Mars orbiter, Phobos lander, and Phobos hovercraft. A ground-control error caused the loss of Phobos 1 in late 1988 and a loss of communication with Phobos 2 in March 1989 caused cancellation of that mission as well.

1992 **Mars Observer** **U.S.** Most thorough orbiter survey of Mars planned to date, scheduled for launch aboard the Shuttle in the fall.

* Indicates a successful mission

Space-Age Mars

The fourth planet from the Sun, Mars falls between the Earth and the Earth's Moon in size. Its mass, however, because of the concentration of lighter elements in its core, is only about 10.7% that of Earth's, and the planet's escape velocity of only 3.17 miles (5.10 km) per second allows the red planet to hold onto only a very thin atmosphere. Measurements of the Martian atmosphere show it to be composed of approximately 95% carbon dioxide, 2.7% nitrogen, 1.6% argon, and traces of other gases, including about 0.15% oxygen. Because, like the Earth, Mars is tilted on its axis of rotation, the planet also has seasons—summer, fall, winter and spring. Its year is 686.9 Earth-days long and its days, at 24 hours, 37 minutes, are just slightly longer than Earth's.

Viewed by telescope from Earth, the seasonal changes on Mars, including the spring shrinking of its north polar cap, had contributed to our pre-space-age vision of the planet as similar in many ways to our own. Maybe it even enjoyed the familiar pattern of seeds sprouting, growing green and then fading and dying with the seasons.

Early Probes and Mariner 4

The space-age exploration of Mars began on October 10 and 14, 1960, when the Soviet Union, long fascinated by the red planet, attempted to launch two small probes toward the distant target. Both attempts failed, as well as a third one two years later. On November 1st, 1962, the Soviets tried again. This time a 1,970-pound probe named Mars 1 was launched successfully and began its long journey to the planet. All seemed in order for a successful flyby when suddenly communications with Earth failed and the probe fell silent shortly before its scheduled encounter. A fifth attempt to launch also fizzled.

So the untouched world of Mars still held its mystery when the United States probe Mariner 3 was launched on November 5, 1964. The U.S. mission, too, would be a failure, though, when a fiberglass shroud used to protect the spacecraft as it traveled through the Earth's atmosphere failed to jettison, trapping its radio antenna and other equipment uselessly beneath it.

Finally, on July 14, 1965, the first robot explorer from Earth streaked across the Martian equator,

A Viking view of Olympus Mons, Mars's great volcano

NASA Jet Propulsion Laboratory

passed over the winter-locked southern hemisphere and began taking pictures. Launched on November 28, 1964 by an Atlas/Agena rocket from Earth, one month and 16 days later the small spacecraft named Mariner 4 arrived where no man—or extension of man—had gone before. A lonely alien visitor 6,082.6 miles (9,788.8 km) above the surface of the planet at its closest approach, Mariner 4 weighed only 575 pounds (260.8 kg) although it contained over 138,000 separate parts. Equipped with six scientific instruments, including an ionization chamber (for measuring ionizing radiation) to count cosmic rays, a "Trapped Radiation detector" to search for a radiation belt similar to Earth's Van Allen belt, a "Cosmic Ray Telescope," a magnetometer to measure the planet's magnetic field, a solar plasma probe (to measure particles coming from the Sun) and a camera, Mariner 4 was poised to give humankind its first close-up look at Mars.

The portrait was not what everyone had hoped for. The instrumentation aboard revealed that Mars had a surface air pressure less than 1% that of Earth's at sea-level (much too low to allow liquid water to exist). Because of the low gravity of Mars much of the atmosphere had long since disappeared into space. It also showed the planet had neither a magnetic field nor radiation belt. The spacecraft's 22 digitized pictures, sent laboriously and slowly back to Earth at a rate of one every 8½ hours, appeared to reveal a planet as dry, cold and lifeless as the Earth's Moon. We would later see that Mars has, perhaps, unlike our Moon, not always been so silent, so cold, so still.

From these images, though, Mars appeared to have no large mountains, valleys, ocean basins or river channels. Ancient and inert beneath a cloudless sky, its surface covered with craters apparently unchanged in millions of years, the Mars of Mariner 4 ended centuries of human dreams.

But if pre-space-age visions of the planet had been wrong, the results of Mariner 4 were also misleading.

In fact, Mariner 4 had covered only about 1% of the planet, certainly not enough to give a complete picture. More would have to be done to bring the true Mars into focus.

Mariner 6 and 7

To do that NASA launched Mariners 6 and 7 back-to-back in February and March of 1969. It was the first planetary double-launch for the United States, and the two craft arrived safely at their destination in July and August of 1969. Fitted out with two cameras instead of the single-camera system used by Mariner 4, Mariners 6 and 7 sent back 201 higher-quality photos of the Martian surface. The new high-resolution pictures gave a better look at the south polar cap and found clouds or haze hovering over the south polar region. They revealed the Martian surface to be much less cratered than the Mariner 4 pictures had suggested, and features in the new photos indicated that some kind of erosion process, the best guess was wind, was occurring on the planet. As other instruments aboard the two craft relayed their data aback to Earth clarifying our estimates of the diameter of the planet and its surface temperatures, the first hints of large mountains and perhaps even volcanoes began to emerge. The image of Mars began to shift again.

Soviet Probes and Mariners 8 and 9

Like a flurry of arrows heading toward their distant target, some hitting some missing, the launches stepped up. The Soviets, whose luck had been running on the bad side in 1971, sent three spacecraft, one unnamed, then Mars 2, and Mars 3, all relatively unsuccessful. The luck of the United States appeared to be running out briefly, too, when a Mariner 8 mission failed and fell into the Atlantic Ocean on May 8th of 1971. On May 30, 1971, however, Mariner 9, NASA's most sophisticated Mars mission up to that time, was launched successfully. Arriving at Mars on November 13, 1971, its larger cameras, higher gain antenna and more sophisticated equipment spent the next three months answering questions that had intrigued observers and scientists for years.

Undaunted and waiting patiently until a dust storm passed, the robot spacecraft "parked" itself in orbit and began relaying its information.

The Mars of Mariner 9 was spectacular.

Where the early missions had seen only cratered and chaotic terrain, Mariner 9 began sending back stunning and, for many, mind-boggling pictures of vast plains, canyons, volcanoes (including a giant twice the size of Earth's Mount Everest) and thousands of small channels.

Far from being an ancient inert world, Mars as seen by the cameras and instruments of Mariner 9 gave every evidence of having been a vital and active planet in the past, a world where once rivers may have flowed and volcanoes erupted—a planet whose surface temperature and atmosphere may once have been different enough to have supported some very simple form of life. As the enormous amount of Mariner 9 data flowed back to Earth, theories were propounded, challenged, discarded, re-analyzed, restructured, tentatively agreed with, scoffed at and endorsed.

What was certain was that Mars was fascinating. A volcano, given the name Olympus Mons, rose to over 79,000 feet above the Martian surface and had a base over 350 miles across, large enough to completely cover the state of Missouri! In addition to having the largest known mountain in the Solar System, Mars also boasted the largest canyon—Valles Marineris—a gigantic rift stretching nearly a sixth of the way around the planet. Nearly 2,800 miles long and at places 370 miles wide, Valles Marineris is nearly 13 times longer than Earth's Grand Canyon. If you stretched it across the United States this huge canyon would reach from New York to California!

A geologist's paradise, photos of the Mars viewed by Mariner 9 also reveal the remains of a gigantic landslide, over 62 miles long, what appears to be ancient, dry river channels, some over 600 miles long and 100 miles wide, and a gigantic asteroid impact basin named Hellas, over 100 miles in diameter.

Once more, science's view of Mars had shifted. Sending over 7,300 pictures of the planet back to Earth, including images of Mars's two small moons, Phobos and Deimos, Mariner 9 was a triumph. It would be a hard act to follow, but the next step for the United States was obvious: a lander to relay pictures back from the planet's surface, with equipment aboard designed to search for any sign of life.

Mars 4, 5, 6 and 7

Meanwhile the Soviets continued their launches with mixed success. Mars 4, launched July 21, 1973, approached Mars on February 19, 1974. Again, though, bad luck plagued the Russians when a failed retrorocket sent the craft astray in the Solar System. Mars 5, launched on July 25, 1973, reached Mars orbit in February of 1974 and managed to get some successful pictures, confirming the volcanoes discovered by the U.S. Mariner 9. Two more Soviet craft, Mars 6 and Mars 7, were then launched on August 5 and 9, 1973. Arriving first at the planet, on March 9, 1974, Mars 7 failed to gain Martian orbit, continuing on to orbit the Sun. Soviet luck changed briefly, however, with Mars 6. Arriving on March 12, 1974, its landing capsule sent back the first direct information on the chemical composition of the atmosphere, revealing carbon dioxide as the major component, before its transmission died just before touching down on the planet's surface.

What excited the world's scientific community, however, were suggestions from the Soviet scientists that, based on the Mars 6 data, the Martian atmosphere contained larger amounts of argon than anticipated. Because argon is a "noble," or inert, gas, which cannot combine with other molecules, many argued that the argon findings could be interpreted to mean that Mars may have had a much denser atmosphere in its distant past—that at one time there had also been larger amounts of other gases that since had either combined with other elements or dissipated. If so, the reasoning goes, perhaps the Martian atmosphere was at one time dense enough to have kept running water on the planet's surface from evaporating.

If the Soviet scientists' suggestions held true, they would reinforce the interpretation of many U.S. scientists that many of the channels cutting across the Martian surface had been caused by running water. If Mars had borne so much water in the past, then wasn't it possible also that it may have supported life? Certainly the observations of the Mariner spacecraft had banished forever any idea of advanced civilization on Mars, either in the present or the past, but life comes in many forms, and perhaps there was yet some type of living organism to be discovered.

Viking: The Robot Scientist

A closer look at Mars was needed. The job was given to an awkward-looking half-billion-dollar spacecraft called Viking. Actually, Viking was not a single spacecraft but two two-part spacecraft, two Viking Orbiters, each combined with a parachute-dropped robot called a Viking Lander. Collectively known as the Viking Project, the small space-faring assemblage was the most elaborate and sophisticated planetary exploration program yet put together by the United States.

The key components of the project were the landers. Released by their respective orbiters and using a combination of retrorockets and parachutes to reach the red planet's surface and begin their work, the landers, looking like a cross between a Volkswagen and a land crab, would give the closest look yet at Mars. A miracle of modern miniaturization, each lander carried two automated chemical laboratories, a weather station, a seismology station, a small photographic lab, two computers, communications equipment, a hoe and shovel for trench digging, and a conveyer system to move collected dirt samples from the robot arm to be analyzed inside the

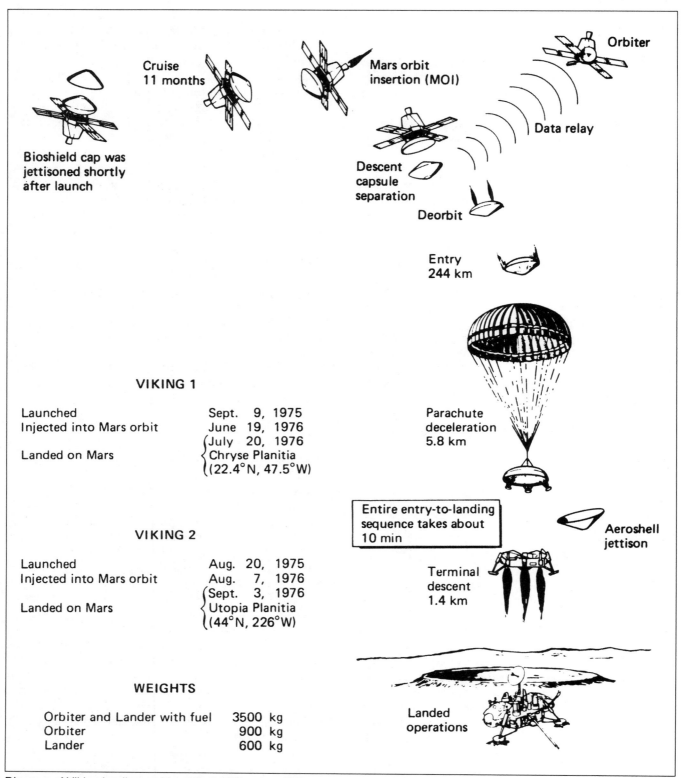

Cruise
11 months

Mars orbit
insertion (MOI)

Orbiter

Data relay

Descent
capsule
separation

Deorbit

Bioshield cap was
jettisoned shortly
after launch

Entry
244 km

Parachute
deceleration
5.8 km

VIKING 1

Launched	Sept. 9, 1975
Injected into Mars orbit	June 19, 1976
Landed on Mars	July 20, 1976 Chryse Planitia (22.4°N, 47.5°W)

Entire entry-to-landing
sequence takes about
10 min

Aeroshell
jettison

Terminal
descent
1.4 km

VIKING 2

Launched	Aug. 20, 1975
Injected into Mars orbit	Aug. 7, 1976
Landed on Mars	Sept. 3, 1976 Utopia Planitia (44°N, 226°W)

Landed
operations

WEIGHTS

Orbiter and Lander with fuel	3500	kg
Orbiter	900	kg
Lander	600	kg

Diagram of Viking landing on Mars. Both Viking 1 and Viking 2 were launched as two-part spacecraft. Once each spacecraft approached Mars, its lander separated from its orbiter as shown and began its descent to the surface, broadcasting signals back to the circling orbiter, which in turn sent them back to Earth

Viking Lander

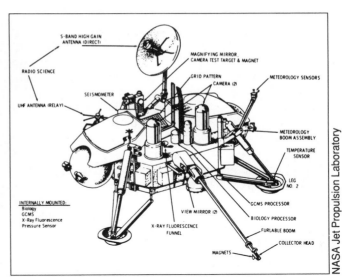

Diagram of a Viking Lander. Both Viking landers carried many scientific instruments to make measurements on the surface of Mars.

lander. All this was packed into a little spindly-looking, three-legged package smaller than a compact car and powered by a tiny 50 watt generator—less power than an average light bulb!

Launched by a Titan 3/Centaur rocket, Viking 1 began its voyage from Earth on August 20, 1975 and arrived at its destination in Mars orbit on June 19, 1976. Viking 2 followed its companion on September 9, 1975 and reached Mars orbit on August 7, 1976.

It had been an uneventful journey and the Viking Project had begun its work when a small hitch in the mission caused a delay in the deployment of the Viking 1 Lander. The initial landing site chosen by scientists after studying the Mariner 9 photographs was discovered by the Viking 1 Orbiter's camera to be too rough for the lander to put down safely. After a 16-day delay while Orbiter cameras and Earth-based radar searched for a new landing site, Viking 1 finally touched down on the planet's surface on July 20, 1976. Viking 2 put down a few weeks later on September 3, 1976, about 4,000 miles away from its robot companion. Although there had been some last minute concern among a small group of scientists that the landers might sink and vanish into soft sand at the landing sites, both landers touched down safely and in working order.

And work is what the two robots had been designed to do.

While the two Viking orbiters circled the planet overhead—running their observing sequences and taking pictures—Lander 1, from its desolate site in a lowland desert called Chryse Planitia, began to send back the first surface-based pictures of the red planet.

Amazingly, after the first black-and-white picture had been made of the rock-strewn ground directly in front of the lander, the first color photos sent back to Earth revealed the sky to be tinted pinkish by dust in the atmosphere. Sometimes, it appeared, Mars really was red—or at least pink!

Sand dunes at Chryse Planitia Basin, as seen by Viking 1

Lander 1 also sent back the first weather report from the Martian surface—light wind at 15 miles (24 km) an hour, and temperatures ranging between −120.5 degrees F (−84.7 degrees C) in the early morning to −21.5 degrees F (−29.7 degrees C) in the afternoon. Fair weather—if a little cold—for a Martian picnic.

Turning to the Martian soil the landers issued their reports back to waiting scientists on Earth. The soil was composed of 15-20% silicon, 14% iron, and traces of calcium, aluminum, sulfur, titanium, magnesium and potassium. The heavy abundance of iron helped to explain the rust-colored tint to the dust in the sky.

While the orbiters continued around the planet, giving the clearest pictures yet of its amazing features and adding fuel to the argument that running water had once existed in quantity on the Martian surface, the landers prepared for their most important experiment.

Since most scientists discounted the idea that the Viking landers' cameras would actually discover any visible sign of life on the planet—anything that might go "walking by"—hope for a solution to the "life on Mars question" was left to three biology experiments assigned to each lander.

The basic idea behind the experiments was to try to incubate living soil organisms by simulated sunlight, water and nutrients. Each computer-controlled lander, acting like a well-trained "robot scientist," used its hoe and shovel to dig a small trench and scoop up some soil. It then transported the soil to its internal laboratories for analysis. As often happens in science, though, the test results were inconclusive. While there was some indication of processes that might have signaled the existence of microscopic Martian life, contradictory results also suggested that some unknown form of inorganic chemical reactions may have provoked the same results. Given the general inhospitability of the Martian environment, and the lack of clear-cut proof of life, most scientists concluded that the evidence pointed to nonbiological processes at work. In short, no signs of life.

Viking Orbiter 2 was shut down by NASA on July 24, 1978 after it ran out of the fuel needed to control its position, or attitude. Orbiter 1 continued taking high-quality pictures and returning scientific data until it also ran out of fuel on August 8, 1980. Attempts to obtain more data from Lander 2 were stopped in March of 1980 after a power failure, and Lander 1, after continuing to send photographs and scientific data for over six years, joined its companion robot in silence in 1983.

Viking 1 soil sampler with completed trench

NASA Jet Propulsion Laboratory

Although life had not been found on Mars, new vigor was given to the study of the red planet as a result of the Viking Project and its Mariner predecessors. No longer the green fertile world of science-fiction writers, nor the inert moon-like world seen by Mariner 4, Mars is now known as a planet with a fascinating history and fascinating mysteries yet to be unraveled. Our view of Mars today is one of a world with an enormously active geological history, a place of gigantic mountains, volcanoes and valleys, a planet that once may have had raging rivers of swiftly moving water and a much denser atmosphere, perhaps even briefly capable of sustaining life.

Phobos: A Marred Flight

High hopes for new insights accompanied the July 1988 launch of the Soviet Phobos mission. It was planned to take an intensive look at Mars and one of its two small and irregular satellites, Phobos. Like its tiny companion satellite, Deimos, Phobos may be a captured asteroid and holds much interest for scientists. The innermost and larger of the two Martian "moons," potato-shaped Phobos measures only 17 by 13.5 by 12 miles (28 by 23 by 20 km) on its three axes and orbits only 3,718 miles (5,983 km) above the Martian surface. Deimos is even smaller—6.8 by 7.4 by 9.3 miles (10 by 12 by 16 km). The Phobos Mission, one of the most ambitious ever planned to the Mars system by the Soviets, was to put two spacecraft into Mars orbit and release two "landers," one to "hop" on the Phobos surface and give us the first close look at one of these strange moons. Unfortunately, both spacecraft failed before reaching Mars, disappointing scientists throughout the world.

Mysteries Yet To Be Solved

If Mars did once have a denser atmosphere, allowing water to exist in liquid form on its surface, where and why has all the water gone? Is some of it locked in permafrost just beneath the planet's surface? Exactly how much is stored permanently frozen as ice at the planet's north pole? We know definitely that some water still exists there. In summer when most of the carbon dioxide ice of the pole has dissipated, a small water ice cap can be seen. The cap itself sits on top of a curiously thick series of layered shelves that may be composed of dust and water ice.

Perhaps there was once swiftly running water that carved out the gigantic Martian channels. Some scientists speculate that possibly a very exotic form of simple life may have existed in the "just maybe" more hospitable Martian past and that we may someday discover some trace, some fossil evidence of that past. Like all good scientists the robot Mars explorers—Viking and its predecessors—have answered many questions but have also posed many more.

Future Missions to Mars

Although the twin Phobos Mission failed, it is only the first of a series of missions planned for Mars over the next dozen years. While the United States studies its scheduled Mars Observer mission, due to be launched in 1992, the Soviets have also announced plans for at least a half-dozen various voyages to the red planet, possibly including a mission that would actually send back soil samples to be examined here on Earth or in Earth orbit.

One of the most exciting possibilities for return missions to Mars—and one of humankind's biggest steps yet into outer space—may be a Soviet manned voyage scheduled sometime after the turn of the century. The United States is also looking into long-range plans for a manned Mars mission—and a joint U.S./USSR manned venture may even lie in the future.

"Mars," in the words of one NASA scientist, "is hot again." The future may hold many more "visions" of the red planet—and, if the past is any indication, some more big surprises.

PART 2

EXPLORING THE OUTER PLANETS

5

JUPITER: THE GIANT PLANET

We're racing through time and space at an incredible rate—the rate at which we are learning things is awe-inspiring in itself.
—Larry Soderblom
Voyager Science Team

It may sound unprofessional but a lot of people up in the imaging team area are just standing around with their mouths hanging open watching the pictures come in . . .
—Brad Smith
Voyager Imaging Team

Past the rocky planets, across the asteroid belt, into a realm of the Solar System far different from that of Earth and its terrestrial neighbors, rules Jupiter, king of the giant planets.

The fifth planet from the Sun, Jupiter is also the largest planet in the Solar System, making up 71% of the mass in the entire system, excluding the Sun itself. It would take more than 1,000 Earths to make up the volume of Jupiter, and the giant planet's diameter is 88,748 miles (142,796 km), 11 times that of Earth's. If you imagined Jupiter as a dinner plate the Earth would be the size of an olive sitting on it.

Jupiter also rotates faster than any other planet on its axis, spinning once every 10 hours. If you could stand on Jupiter's equator you would find yourself traveling at a heady 27,720 mph (44,611 kph).

It would be impossible, though, for humans to stand on Jupiter because the planet has no solid surface. With a composition very similar to the Sun's—89% hydrogen and 11% helium—and an average density of only 1.3 times that of water, Jupiter is a giant gaseous sphere, probably with a liquid interior.

Taking 12 Earth years to orbit the Sun, the planetary Goliath is one of the most intriguing and colorful of all the objects in our Solar System.

Historical Jupiter

One of the most easily observable of what the Greeks called the "wandering stars" or planets, Jupiter has commanded the attention of humankind throughout history. Named for the greatest of all the Roman gods (Jupiter, sometimes called Jove), the planet was one of the first to be studied by telescope. Its importance in the history of human thought was forever established in 1610 when Galileo, turning his small telescope toward the heavens, discovered Jupiter's four major satellites and found the first clear proof of celestial objects orbiting a common center.

During the 1940s and 1950s, gathering together all the evidence of Earth-based observations, astronomers began to put together our modern view

Jupiter: The Planet

Position: Fifth from Sun
Average Distance from Sun: 483.7 million miles (778.3 million km)—compared to Earth at 92.95 million miles (149.59 million km)
Diameter: 88,748 miles (142,796 km), 11.23 times the size of Earth
Mass: 318 times Earth's
Density: 1.32 (Water = 1)
Volume: 1,317 times Earth's
Surface Gravity: 2.64 times Earth's
Period of Rotation on Axis: Once every 9.8 Earth hours
Revolution around Sun: Once every 11.9 Earth years (sidereal period)
Orbital Speed: 8.14 miles/sec (13.1 km/sec)
Satellites: 16

A montage of Voyager photos of Jupiter and its Galilean moons, Io, Europa, Ganymede and Callisto

NASA Jet Propulsion Laboratory

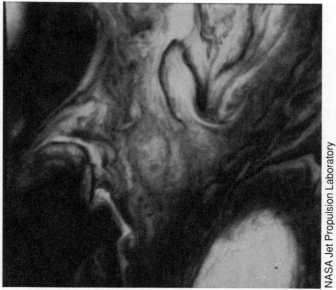

NASA Jet Propulsion Laboratory

Closeup of the turbulent clouds of Jupiter, the great gas giant

of this celestial giant. Encouraged by the German-American astronomer Rupert Wildt, a spectacular new understanding of the majestic planet began to emerge.

The most strikingly obvious fact to surface during this pre-space age period was that the giant planet was more like the Sun than it was like the Earth. Although Earth and the inner planets in the Solar System (those inside the asteroid belt and closest to the Sun) are small rocky bodies with few if any satellites, planets

Reaching Out to the Giant:
Missions to Jupiter

1972   Pioneer 10   U.S.   Launched March 3, at a dazzling speed of 32,400 mph (52,143 kph) Pioneer 10 was the first probe to cross the asteroid belt, arriving at the Jovian system on December 3, 1973. It provided the first close-up photos of Jupiter's Great Red Spot and its moons.

1973   Pioneer 11   U.S.   Twin to Pioneer 10, this probe was launched more than a year later on April 5, 1973 to perform the same mission via a different trajectory, arriving at Jupiter December 3, 1974. From there Pioneer 11 veered on to Saturn.

1977   Voyager 1 and 2   U.S.   Launched on August 20, Voyager 2 was followed by its twin, Voyager 1, a few days later on September 5. Voyager 1, however, played catch-up to arrive at Jupiter four months earlier on March 5, 1979, with the second in the team reaching the Jovian system on July 9. Together they sent back spectacular images of the satellites, plus close-ups of the Jovian ring system, as well as the Great Red Spot. They also measured the giant magnetosphere of Jupiter, the largest in the solar system. Both Voyagers went on to Saturn and beyond, with Voyager 2 visiting Uranus in 1986 and Neptune in 1989.

1989   Galileo   U.S.   An orbiter/probe combined mission to the Jovian system, slated to arrive in 1995. The probe should give us the first on-site data about the atmosphere of Jupiter itself and the orbiter will take a two-year "grand tour" of the giant planet's satellite system.

farther from the Sun are for the most part composed of different stuff altogether. With the exception of little-known Pluto, the outer planets are gas giants, composed primarily of the simplest elements, hydrogen and helium. Most of these outer planets also have an extensive system of satellites. And, as recent explorations have revealed, all four of the gas giants—Saturn, Jupiter, Uranus and Neptune—also possess

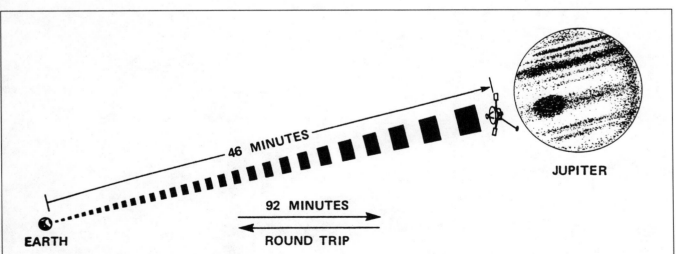

Radio waves from a spacecraft at Jupiter take 46 minutes to travel to Earth—so a ground crew sending instructions receives no reply for more than an hour and a half

rings. Taking these major differences between the inner and outer planets into account, modern scientists began to understand Jupiter as a planet with a history much different from Earth's.

Created primarily from the same basic materials that formed the nebula out of which our Solar System was born nearly 4.5 billion years ago, Jupiter and the other giant planets grew very rapidly, and their strong gravity helped them hold onto their original matter. The chemical elements that "built" Jupiter were "sunlike" in nature and remained so. Although born in the same nebula, however, Earth and the inner planets, perhaps because they grew more slowly, couldn't hold onto light gases like hydrogen and helium effectively. So, the two groups proceeded along different cosmological paths.

But if Jupiter was a body very similar to the Sun and other stars in its compositional make-up, why hadn't it burst forth and become a star?

The answer again lies in Jupiter's size. Although large enough to have retained its star-like composition, it was not large enough to have begun those

nuclear reactions deep inside its body that would have triggered its stellar burst. Yet ground-based observations early established that Jupiter puts out much more energy, as evidenced by its luminosity, or brightness, than it receives from the Sun (as we'd also later discover about its giant neighbor Saturn). This strange phenomenon is probably due to a combination of leftover energy from the planet's original formation, gravitational contraction and other processes that produce tremendous heat within. Still, impressive in its majestic size but never able to grow massive enough to ignite with solar warmth, Jupiter held onto its large family of satellites.

Space-Age Jupiter

The space-age study of Jupiter began on March 3, 1972, when the U.S. launched Pioneer 10, the first spacecraft to cross the asteroid belt and make close observations of the Jupiter system.

Boosted by Atlas/Centaur rockets and weighing only 570 pounds (259 kg), the tiny Pioneer 10, like its sister craft Pioneer 11 launched a year later, packed a

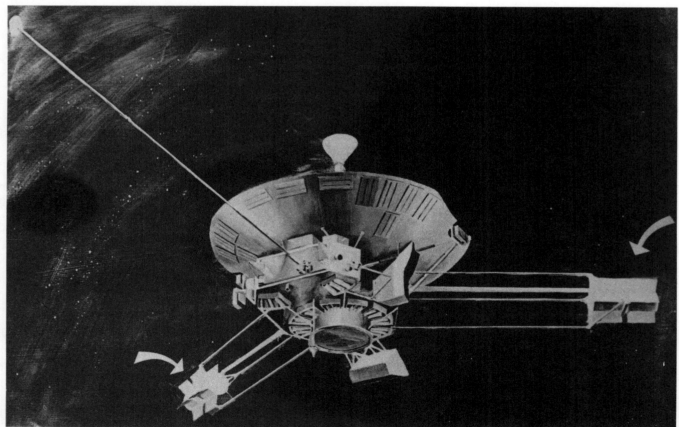

NASA

Artist's conception of the Pioneer spacecraft that went to Jupiter. The nuclear generators used by the spacecraft for power on their long voyage are indicated by arrows

powerhouse of instrumentation in its small body. Designed to conduct the first flyby of an outer planet, it carried on board a meteoroid detector, meteoroid/asteroid detector, radio, plasma analyzer, charged- particle detector, cosmic ray telescope, ultraviolet photometer, infrared radiometer and many other sophisticated instruments. All this in a tiny 9-foot-by-14-inch (2.7 m x 35.5 cm) equipment compartment!

Although there were initial worries that the spacecraft might be damaged as it flew past the asteroid belt, it negotiated its course unscathed and passed the orbital paths of Jupiter's outer moons in early November 1973. On November 26, Pioneer 10 switched on its cameras and began its survey of Jupiter and its satellites Callisto, Europa and Ganymede, making its closest approach to Jupiter (81,000 miles; 130,350 km) on December 3. Disappointingly, Pioneer 10 could not obtain photos of the fourth major satellite, Io. Observing Jupiter closer than ever before, Pioneer 10 confirmed Earth-based observations by finding no solid surface beneath the thick clouds of the planet. It explored Jupiter's magnetosphere and made close-up pictures of the Great Red Spot and other features of the Jovian atmosphere. It also made measurements at relatively close range of all four major satellites and mapped the heliosphere, magnetic field and solar wind.

Launched on April 5, 1973 and outfitted with instrumentation similar to its sister craft's, Pioneer 11 set out to fly much closer to Jupiter and continue on to a flyby of Saturn. After passing safely through the asteroid belt it made its closest approach (26,680 miles; 42,936 km) below Jupiter's south pole on December 3, 1974. Pioneer 11 took more detailed but still fuzzy pictures of the planet and its satellites, and made the first study of its north and south poles, which were unobservable from the Earth.

Pioneer Results

While relatively simple by today's spacecraft standards, the two Pioneer Jupiter spacecraft gave scientists the first close-up look at the giant planet and its satellites. Although the soon-to-follow and much better equipped Voyager spacecraft would astound the world with their transmissions from the Jupiter system, Pioneers 10 and 11 were just that—pioneers—and scientists were justly proud of their scientific achievements.

Among the collective discoveries of Pioneers 10 and 11 was the insight that the magnetic field of the planet is the reverse of Earth's and that the strength of the solar wind doesn't weaken on its way toward

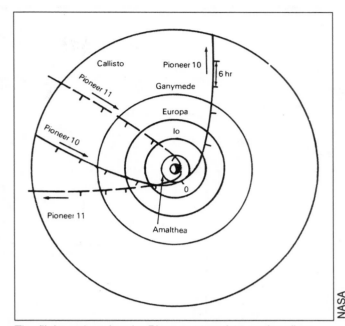

The flight paths taken by Pioneer 10 and 11 as they flew through the Jupiter system

the outer planets. Jupiter was also discovered to be a source of strong magnetic particle emission—a huge magnetosphere or area where the planet's magnetic field dominates that of the Sun.

The first pictures of Jupiter showed it to be a world in swirling, turbulent motion, greatly flattened at its poles. Measuring the Great Red Spot on the face of the planet to be nearly 24,000 miles (38,623 km) across, the Pioneers also examined another smaller red spot in the northern hemisphere. As a result scientists could see that both the large and small spots are semipermanent hurricanes swirling furiously counterclockwise.

Examination of the rest of the atmosphere revealed it to be close to what scientists had thought—mostly hydrogen and helium, plus a small percentage of other gases. These and other observations lead scientists to believe that Jupiter's interior is probably mostly liquid and that its central temperature may range from 22,890 to 62,490 degrees F (12,700 to 34,700 degrees C). With a central pressure probably 100 million times the pressure of the Earth's atmosphere, this interior is probably ultracompressed hydrogen that may surround a rocky core. Scientists believe that at the lower levels, liquid hydrogen takes the form of molecules that have been stripped of their outer electrons and are thus "metallic" and able to conduct heat and electricity. It is probably within these areas that the planet's intense magnetic field is generated.

Messages from Earth

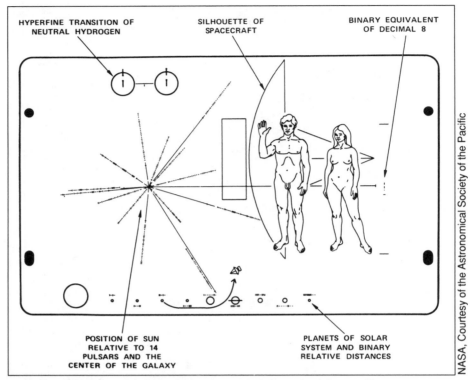

A plaque etched with these symbols was carried on each of the two Pioneer spacecraft. On the right, a man and a woman of our species stand in front of an outline of the spacecraft. (Note that the facial features bear traits from all three major races of humanity.) At the bottom is a diagram of our Solar System, showing the flight path of the spacecraft launched from Earth past Jupiter and Saturn, and then outward into the far reaches of space

Crossing the boundaries of the Solar System and journeying into the dark reaches of space, Pioneers 10 and 11 and Voyagers 1 and 2 all carry with them poignant messages for unknown receivers. Like bottles tossed into the cosmic ocean from our small island in space, each message carries with it humankind's announcement of its presence in the vastness of the universe.

The Pioneers carry identical etched gold-anodized aluminum plates 6 by 9 inches in size and 0.05 inches thick that identify humankind's place in the universe in time and space. Carrying images of the male and female form standing in front of a silhouette of the Pioneer spacecraft, the plaques also carry symbols identifying our position in space relative to 14 pulsars and the center of the Milky Way Galaxy. Other symbols represent neutral hydrogen and the planets of our Solar System with their relative distances.

More ambitiously, and perhaps even more hopefully, the two Voyager spacecraft carry phonograph records (with needles and cartridges to play them), packed full of the sounds and images of planet Earth and its inhabitants. The 12-inch gold-plated copper disks encased in protective aluminum jackets each hold 115 coded images of earthly scenes ranging from sand dunes and forests to the structure of DNA and the Golden Gate Bridge. Each record also contains greetings spoken in 60 different languages, and more than 35 sounds familiar on Earth, such as human laughter, birds singing, elephants trumpeting, lift-off of a Saturn 2 rocket, the pounding surf and a baby crying. Over two dozen musical selections ranging from Beethoven to Chuck Berry round out Voyagers' portrayal of the diversity of life and culture on Earth.

Will these cosmic messages be picked up by others somewhere, sometime, in the great vastness of space? The chances, most agree, are slim. Imagine the odds against two ants meeting by chance in the center of the pitcher's mound of Wrigley Field in Chicago if one were released in New York and the other in San Francisco. Still, if a million years from now such an unlikely chance encounter should occur, and Pioneer or Voyager falls into the hands (tentacles, claws, or whatsits) of a friendly alien, one more message will ring loud and clear—humankind is a wonderfully optimistic and questing species.

The two spacecraft also revealed that Jupiter's clouds are composed mostly of condensed ammonia compounds and water and that their red, yellow and rust colors are probably due to these ammonia compounds reacting to the ultraviolet light of the Sun.

The Voyagers

Launched in 1977 and programmed to explore the outer bodies of the Solar System, Voyagers 1 and 2 were much more sophisticated spacecraft than their Pioneer predecessors. Boosted by powerful Titan 3/Centaur rockets and carrying a total weight of 46,000 pounds (20,866 kg), including 230 pounds (104 kg) of scientific equipment, the Voyager spacecraft were state-of-the-art for American technology. For their scientific payload each craft carried a radio science experiment and 10 scientific instruments, including an infrared spectrometer and radiometer, ultraviolet spectrometer, and two television cameras for higher resolution imaging and many other highly sophisticated instruments for studying astrophysics and astronomy.

Using a unique planetary alignment, Voyager 1 was launched September 5, 1977, and arrived at the Jupiter system in March 1979. With a trajectory that took it near Callisto, Ganymede, Europa and Io, it made its closest encounter with Jupiter (17,400 miles; 28,000 km) on March 5, 1979. Then, using a gravity assist from Jupiter to sling-shot on its way, it headed toward Saturn and a fresh round of observations there. Voyager 2, its sister craft, was actually

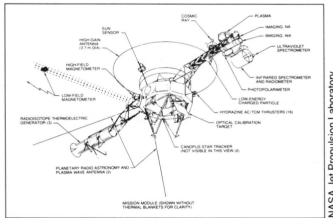

Voyager spacecraft

NASA Jet Propulsion Laboratory

launched earlier, on August 20, 1977, but reached Jupiter four months later, in July 1979. Voyager 2 passed near Callisto, Ganymede and Europa and took a look at one of its smallest and innermost satellites, Amalthea, before its closest observations of Jupiter on July 9, 1979.

Scientific Returns from Voyager

A spectacular success, the Voyager program during its Jupiter encounter unveiled, quite literally, "worlds of wonder" to enthralled scientists.

Kicking its cameras into action a year after entering the asteroid belt and sending photos back to Earth at the relatively "close" range of 31 million miles (50

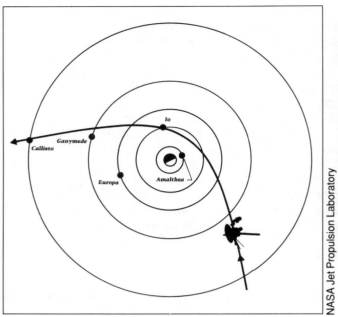

Voyager 1 flight path near Jupiter

NASA Jet Propulsion Laboratory

The exciting discovery of volcanoes on Io was made by optical navigation engineer Linda Morabito and her colleagues from this photo taken by Voyager 1

NASA Jet Propulsion Laboratory, Courtesy of the Astronomical Society of the Pacific

million km) from Jupiter, Voyager 1 opened the spectacular show with the first close-up high-resolution pictures of the Jovian system.

Among its most exciting and unexpected discoveries was the first currently volcanically active world besides the Earth to be discovered in the Solar System.

Io: The Volcanic Surprise

Io is the innermost of the four great satellites (named "Galilean" as a group after their discoverer, 17th-century Italian astronomer Galileo Galilei). With a diameter of 2,257 miles (3,632 km), Io is the most dense of the Galileans with a density close to that of Earth's Moon. A unique and violently beautiful world with its surface of brilliant reds and yellows punctuated by dozens of jet-black volcanoes, it is the showpiece of Jupiter's satellite system.

Scientists believe that the beautiful crust of Io is actually a layer of solid sulfur 12 miles (19.3 km) thick that may float on a sea of molten sulfur. Tidal attraction by Jupiter may cause this crust to rise and fall as much as 60 miles (96 km). Bursting through this heaving and churning crust, Io's active volcanoes spurt sulfurous material forth at speeds of up to 3,280 miles per second (5,278 km/sec) as far as 174 miles (280 km) high and splash over 100 billion tons of sulfur deposits back on the satellite's surface each year! To complete the volcanic scenario, scientists

also believe that ionized matter—sulfur, oxygen and hydrogen—escape from Io to form a torus, a sort of "donut" of material, centered on the satellite and encompassing the whole of its orbit. Interacting in ways still to be studied with Jupiter's magnetosphere, the torus probably affects the rate at which Jupiter radiates energy and accounts for other phenomena such as bursts of radio waves and auroras on the parent planet.

Rings and Things

The second of Voyager 1's major discoveries was that, like Saturn and Uranus, Jupiter also has a ring system. Dipping within the orbit of Amalthea, the spacecraft found the outer edge of the ring to be about 34,000 miles (54,700 km) above the planet's cloud tops. Believed to be about 3,700 miles (5,950 km) wide and only about 0.6 of a mile (1 km) thick, Jupiter's ring is actually composed of two parts, a bright 500-mile-wide band and a dimmer section about 3,200 miles (5,150 km) wide. Like the much larger and more spectacular rings of Saturn, Jupiter's ring is probably composed of material ranging in size from the microscopic to many feet across. So tenuous is Jupiter's ring, though, that if you could scoop up all the material that encircles the giant planet and dump it into a huge compactor, it would only be a little larger in size than Amalthea, with a diameter of about 93 miles (149 km).

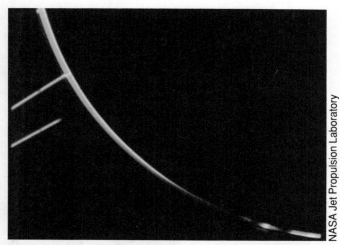

Jupiter's ring seen in sunlight coming from behind the planet

NASA Jet Propulsion Laboratory

The combined observations of Voyagers 1 and 2 resulted in over 35,000 photos and bits of data on Jupiter and its satellites, including the discovery of three more Jovian moons, bringing the total to 16 now known. In addition, the spacecraft took high-resolu-tion close-ups of the Great Red Spot, and discovered cloud-top lightning bolts and auroras similar to Earth's northern lights. And they confirmed the exist-ence of a much higher electric current between Jupiter and Io than predicted. Perhaps the greatest drama provided by the Voyager spacecraft, though, was the unfolding story of Jupiter's "other worlds."

Other Worlds

Jupiter's satellites can be divided up into three separate and distinct groups: the outer group, Ananke, Carme, Pasiphae and Sinope, which move in loosely bound and eccentric orbits of about 700 days; an intermediate group of small satellites—Leda, Himalia, Lysithea and Elara—that move in ap-proximately 250-day orbits; and the inner group, the well-known, large Galileans—Io, Europa, Ganymede and Callisto—along with Amalthea. The Voyagers also discovered Thebe, Adrastea and Metis, which occupy nearly circular orbits close to the planet's equatorial plane.

The Voyagers' charge was to take a closer look at the four giant Galileans. And although dynamic Io

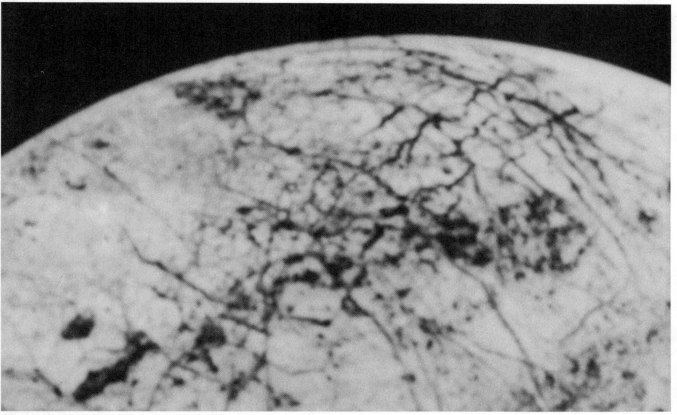

Closeup of Europa, smallest of the Galilean moons, seen at a distance of 150,000 miles (241,395 km)

NASA Jet Propulsion Laboratory

stole the show for many, the other three also offered their share of excitement.

Europa

The smallest of the Galilean satellites at only 1,945 miles (3,130 km) in diameter (just slightly larger than Earth's Moon), Europa appears to be entirely covered with a thin water ice. The moon most certainly has a large rocky core, with possibly a slushy or more liquid layer between the core and the icy surface. Europa's most striking features, though, are a complex series of criss-crossed linear marks that mar its icy smoothness. Sometimes stretching for as far as 600 miles (960 km), these lines seem to be cracks in the icy surface, but do not appear to be crevices. Most look more like someone had taken a pale-colored felt-tip pen and scribbled over the face of a white billiard ball. While fractures in the crust are the best-guess explanation for the curious pattern, their exact nature and the mechanism for their creation is not yet known.

Ganymede

The largest of the Galilean satellites, with a diameter of about 3,275 miles (5,270 km; about one and a half times the size of Earth's Moon), Ganymede is also the brightest moon in the Jovian system. Although its low density suggests that its bulk composition is roughly half water and half rock, Ganymede curiously shows signs of an active geological history. As revealed by the Voyager cameras, Ganymede's surface is com-

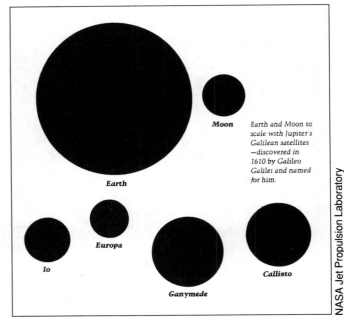

Earth and Moon to scale with Jupiter's Galilean satellites —discovered in 1610 by Galileo Galilei and named for him.

NASA Jet Propulsion Laboratory

Earth and the Moon compared to the Galilean satellites

plexly diverse. Splashed with many dark and heavily cratered areas, probably dating back to the time of its great bombardment 4 billion years ago, the moon also reveals much lighter areas consisting of many parallel lines of mountains and valleys of much more recent origin.

It's believed that Ganymede's curious surface is probably the result of tectonic activity. Current theory holds that, much like the Earth's rocky crust, Ganymede's 60-mile (96-km)-thick icy crust is broken into plates that slide and shift against each other along fracture zones, creating geological activity much like Earth's.

Callisto

The most distant of Jupiter's major moons, Callisto is over 1,170,041 miles (1,882, 947 km) from its parent planet. It has the lowest density of the Galilean satellites. Like Ganymede, it is most likely composed of water ice and rock in nearly equal proportions. Unlike Ganymede, though, Callisto shows no sign of an active geological history and its thick, icy crust (possibly as much as 150 miles (240 km) deep) is the most heavily cratered in the Solar System. In fact its surface is so heavily pockmarked that a meteorite impacting today would have no uncratered area to disturb but would simply superimpose itself over a previous impact crater. A cold, dead and ancient world, Callisto bears silent and sobering evidence to the colossal

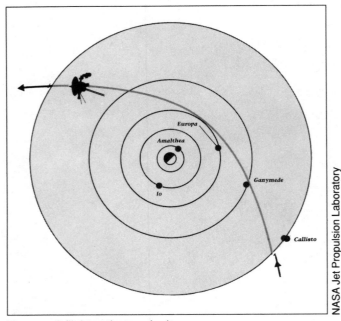

NASA Jet Propulsion Laboratory

Voyager 2 flight path near Jupiter

Satellites of Jupiter

Name	Diameter	Distance from Planet
1979J3	25 miles (40 km)	79,550 miles (128,020 km)
Adrastea (1971J1)	25 miles (40 km)	79,860 miles (128,520 km)
Amalthea	150 miles (240 km)	112,650 miles (181,300 km)
1979J2	50 miles (80 km)	137,780 miles (221,725 km)
Io	2,262 miles (3,640 km)	261,950 miles (421,600 km)
Europa	1,945 miles (3,130 km)	416,900 miles (670,900 km)
Ganymede	3,275 miles (5,270 km)	664,900 miles (1,070,000 km)
Callisto	3,007 miles (4,840 km)	1,170,000 miles (1,880,000 km)
Leda	1.3 to 8.5 miles (2 to 14 km)	6,903,500 miles (11,110,000 km)
Himalia	110 miles (170 km)	7,127,000 miles (11,470,000 km)
Lysithea	3.7 to 20 miles (6 to 32 km)	7,276,000 miles (11,710,000 km)
Elara	50 miles (80 km)	7,295,000 miles (11,740,000 km)
Ananke	3.7 to 17 miles (6 to 28 km)	12,863,000 miles (20,700,000 km)
Carme	5 to 25 miles (8 to 40 km)	13,888,000 miles (22,350,000 km)
Pasiphae	5 to 28.5 miles (8 to 46 km)	14,478,000 miles (23,300,000 km)
Sinope	3.7 to 22 miles (6 to 36 km)	14,727,000 miles (23,700,000 km)

bombardments of impacting objects early in the history of the Jovian system.

Mysteries Still Remaining

As brilliantly successful as the two-part Voyager mission to Jupiter proved to be, the complex Jovian system still holds many mysteries. To list only a few of the most important: What actually lies beneath Jupiter's clouds and what causes their vivid colors? Are present theories about Jupiter's interior correct? Why is the Great Red Spot red? Why are Callisto and Ganymede, though neighbors, so different from one another? Are our theories about volcanic Io really correct? And, finally, what caused those mysterious Europan lines?

Future Missions: At Long Last Galileo

Beginning what NASA scientists call a new "golden age" of space exploration, the U.S. Galileo spacecraft should go a long ways toward answering many of the Jovian mysteries.

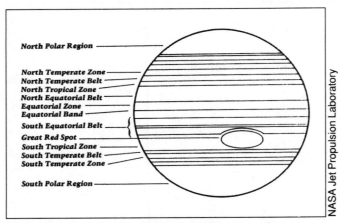

North Polar Region

North Temperate Zone
North Temperate Belt
North Tropical Zone
North Equatorial Belt
Equatorial Zone
Equatorial Band
South Equatorial Belt
Great Red Spot
South Tropical Zone
South Temperate Belt
South Temperate Zone

South Polar Region

NASA Jet Propulsion Laboratory

Many mysteries about Jupiter's atmosphere remain—perhaps the Galileo Jupiter Probe will provide some new answers

Spending two years in a complicated orbit that will allow it to closely study Jupiter and its four major satellites, Galileo will take an even more detailed look at the Jovian system than the sophisticated Voyager missions that preceded it.

The most complex unmanned mission to another planet in the history of the United States space program, the Galileo Project has also been the most troublesome. Originally planned in 1977, Galileo was to have been launched from the Space Shuttle on a direct trajectory to Jupiter. Delays in building the Space Shuttle and booster problems stalled Galileo, however. Then the U.S. halted Shuttle launches for

two and a half years after the Challenger tragedy (when, in the worst disaster in space history, a Shuttle orbiter exploded seconds after launch, killing the entire crew of seven), and Galileo's launch plans changed yet again.

At last its successful launch aboard the Shuttle orbiter Atlantis in October 1989 sent Galileo on its way, maneuvering a complicated trajectory of multiple gravity assists on its course to the giant planet. On its journey Galileo will now pass by Venus and two asteroids, swinging back around Earth twice before arriving at its destination in early December 1995. In the complicated journey, which project scientists call the "VEEGA" route (for Venus-Earth-Earth-Gravity Assist), Galileo passes within 9,300 miles (14,880 km) of Venus in early February 1990, returns within 620 miles (992 km) of Earth in December 1990, skips more than halfway to Jupiter and into the asteroid belt, and then drops back again toward Earth to capture enough gravitational energy to push toward its Jovian target.

Having finally arrived at its destination, Galileo will unpackage an atmospheric probe to be dropped by special parachute into Jupiter's cloud cover. At the same time the orbiter will begin a two-year highly detailed orbital investigation of the Jovian system. Like the Pioneers and Voyagers before it, and like all of humankind's probes into the mysteries of the universe, Galileo promises to send back both solutions and surprises, answers to old mysteries and the first hints of many new ones.

6

SATURN: JEWEL TO THE EYE

What might we want of that giant primal ball of gases? What might we find upon it?
—Roger Zelazny
Science fiction writer

Floating in the night sky like a bright jewel circled by its beautiful rings, Saturn somehow gladdens the heart. In the forest of the night, as small telescopes search the heavens, its sight suggests at once the beauty and mystery of the universe. Once seen through the eyepiece of an amateur's telescope it can never be forgotten, making for a brief while scientists of us all. How and why, we ask, could such a wonder be?

"... The weakness of my understanding, and the fear of being mistaken, have greatly confounded me," Galileo wrote to a friend in 1612. He was greatly perplexed by a mystery his telescope had picked out of the heavens. Two years before, in 1610, he had discovered two strange satellites around Saturn. Unlike Jupiter's moons, though, the objects around Saturn appeared permanently fixed, never moving or changing in relationship to each other or their parent planet. But the mystery that presented itself in 1612 was stranger still. The moons were gone! Vanished! What had happened, of course, was that in 1610 Galileo had seen the rings of Saturn nearly edge-on through his small telescope, making the small portion visible appear to be stationary satellites of the great planet. Looking again in 1612, with the thin rings fully edge-on in relationship to the Earth, Galileo was unable to see them at all.

"Has Saturn perhaps devoured his own children?" Galileo wrote perplexedly. However, while Galileo's observation did call to mind myths of the Roman gods

Saturn and three of its moons, Tethys, Dione and Rhea

NASA Jet Propulsion Laboratory

(Saturn was named after the father of the god Jupiter), certainly this finding didn't fit into Galileo's more scientific view of the universe.

Galileo never solved his mystery, and moved on instead to other problems, but in 1655 an astute Dutch astronomer by the name of Christiaan Huygens became the first to identify Saturn's rings. Huygens, who is also credited with the discovery of one of Saturn's major satellites, Titan, actually believed the rings to be one single flat "ring." It wasn't until Giovanni Domenico Cassini, a French astronomer, though Italian-born, announced his discoveries in 1675 that

Saturn: The Planet

Position: Sixth from Sun
Average Distance from Sun: 886.7 million miles (1,427 million km)—
   9.5388 astronomical AU, compared to Earth's 1 AU, or 92.95 million
   miles (149.59 million km)
Diameter: 74,977 miles (120,660 km), 9.46 times the size of Earth
Mass: 95.2 times Earth's
Density: 0.70 (Water = 1)
Volume: 815 times Earth's
Surface Gravity: 1.13 times Earth's
Period of Rotation on Axis: Once every 10 hours, 14 minutes
Revolution around Sun: Once every 29.5 Earth years (sidereal period)
Orbital Speed: 6.03 miles/sec (9.7 km/sec)
Satellites: 18, plus rings (see boxes)

the planet was recognized as having more than one ring.

Saturn's prestigious place in the Solar System rests on more than its intriguing and beautiful rings, though. The sixth planet from the Sun, taking 29.46 years to complete its orbit, it is the furthest planet from Earth to be observable by the naked eye and second only to Jupiter in size. Curiously, with a diameter of nearly 74,977 miles (120,660 km) and a volume large enough to hold almost 1,000 Earth-sized planets, its density is the lowest of all of the known planets, only 70% the density of water. The whole planet could float quite literally in a giant bathtub!

Space Age Saturn: Pioneer 11

Although Saturn has been studied for years through large and small telescopes, it wasn't until the dawning of the space age that humankind could more closely examine the great ringed planet. The first spacecraft to reach Saturn was the hearty little Pioneer 11, arriving in the Saturn system in August 1979. Traveling at nearly 39,700 miles (63,889 km) per hour it had taken the tiny spacecraft over four years to cover the distance between the two great planets. Designed for a flyby of Saturn, Pioneer 11 made its closest approach 13,300 miles (21,404 km) above the planet's cloud tops on September 1, 1979. Although not designed for an in-depth study of the ringed planet, Pioneer 11 began relaying its information back to Earth, 85 light minutes away.

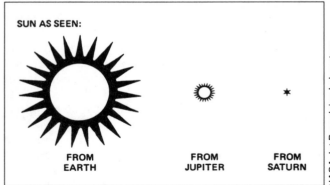

Twice as far from the Sun as Jupiter, Saturn receives only one-fourth as much of the Sun's energy and is a far, far colder place.

During its brief stay, Pioneer 11 gave scientists not only their first close-up look at the planet, its rings and some of its satellites, but also identified two more rings, took a close reading of Saturn's magnetic field and made a rough determination of the planet's mass. The Pioneer instruments revealed the planet's magnetic field to be nearly 1,000 times stronger than Earth's but about 20 times weaker than Jupiter's. Pioneer also registered the first proof of radiation belts, primarily comprised of energetic electrons and protons, around the planet.

The new information indicated that the planet, composed mostly of hydrogen and helium, probably had a central core of heavy elements and an outer core of compressed liquid gases, including methane, ammonia and water. (Substances that normally take the form of gases, when compressed, become liquid.) Best guesses suggested that deep inside the giant's mass the hydrogen was probably in a highly pressurized liquid metallic state.

The Pioneer data indicated Saturn's average surface temperature was a very cold −279 degrees F (−173 degrees C), with an even colder −328 degrees F (−200 degrees C) in the rings, backing up a previously held theory that the rings were probably composed mostly of ice.

By the time Pioneer 11 obtained a fuzzy picture of Titan and began to move out of the Saturn system and head for deep space it had given Earth-bound scientists enough intriguing information to whet their appetites for the better-equipped Voyager investigation yet to come.

Voyager Takes a Closer Look

Arriving at the Saturn system a year after Pioneer 11's departure, Voyager 1 began its investigations of the giant planet in August 1980. Between Voyager 1's first photographs of the planet on August 22, 1980, and its departure from the system December 15 of that same year, it would make its closest approach to Saturn's cloud tops at 78,300 miles (126,000 km) and send back over 17,500 high-quality pictures and millions of bits of new information about the Saturn system.

Its mission partner, Voyager 2, arrived in the summer of 1981 and would make its closest approach to Saturn on August 26 of that year (at 62,760 miles, or 101,000 km, from the cloud tops). Together the two Voyagers would give excited scientists the fullest picture to date of the varied and intriguing Saturn system. By the time of Voyager 2's departure in the autumn of 1981, the Voyager mission had returned a combined total of over 70,000 pictures of Saturn, its rings and satellites, and enough scientific information to mark the billion-dollar Voyager mission as a resounding success.

A Giant Ball of Atmosphere

The Voyager mission to Saturn confirmed Pioneer 11's original observations. Like Jupiter, Saturn is indeed a giant ball of atmosphere. And like Jupiter, Saturn is composed primarily of elements left over from the original formation of the Solar System. Large enough and far enough from the Sun to hold on to its original gases, Saturn today still retains its early primitive composition.

Although Voyager 1 photographs were hampered by a layer of haze, Voyager 2 obtained much clearer views of the planet. Looking through the Voyagers' remote eyes, scientists saw a planet with much less color than the striking contrasts seen on Jupiter. Since Saturn is colder, it is subject to different chemical reactions. The Voyagers also gave scientists their first close views of turbulence in the belts and zones of

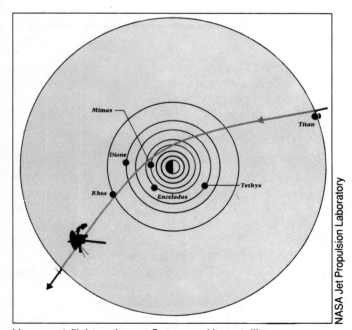

Voyager 1 flight path past Saturn and its satellites

NASA Jet Propulsion Laboratory

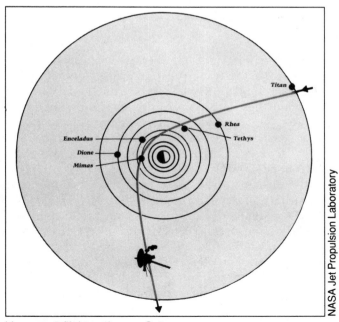

Voyager 2 flight path near Saturn

NASA Jet Propulsion Laboratory

Saturn's Rings

D-ring	With the inner edge of the innermost ring orbiting only 41,630 miles (67,000 km) from the planet's center, Saturn's ring system begins just a little more than 4,000 miles (6,437 km) above the surface, some 2,000 miles (3,218 km) above the cloud tops. The faint D-ring is seen only in forward-scattering light.
C-ring	One of the first three rings to be discovered, the C-ring's inner edge lies 45,500 miles (73,200 km) from Saturn's center.
B-Ring	Nearly 16,000 miles (26,000 km) wide, the bright B-ring's inner edge orbits 57,300 miles (92,200 km) from the planet's center. The outer edge, which marks the inner boundary of the Cassini Division, lies 73,000 miles (117,500 km) from the center.
Cassini Division	A 2,200-mile (3,540-km) break between the B-ring and the A-ring
A-ring, Encke Division	Bounded by the Cassini Division on its inner edge, the A-ring begins at a distance of 75,200 miles (121,000 km) from the planet's center. It's split by the narrow 124-mile (200 km) Encke Division, picks up again, and extends out to a distance 84,600 miles (136,200 km) from the center.
F-ring	At a distance of 87,400 miles (140,600 km), the narrow F-ring is about 62 miles wide (100 km), and is composed of three partly "plaited" strands, probably influenced by satellites 13 and 14.
G-ring	Extremely faint and seen only in forward-scattering light, the G-ring lies 105,600 miles (170,000 km) from Saturn's center.
E-ring	Nearly 50,000 miles (80,465 km) wide, the E-ring encompasses the orbits of both Tethys and Enceladus. Its inner edge lies 130,500 miles (210,000 km) from the planet's center.

Saturn's atmosphere and a series of small white spots that were actually storms in high-pressure regions of Saturn's clouds. Although its lack of obvious swirling colors makes Saturn appear much more placid than Jupiter, Voyager also measured winds on the planet that reached 1,118 miles (1,800 km) per hour, four times higher than those found on Saturn's more flamboyant neighbor.

By measuring bursts of radiation issuing from Saturn's liquid metallic core, scientists were also able to get a tighter fix on Jupiter's magnetic field and determine a rotation rate for the planet of 10 hours and 39 minutes. The Voyagers also verified that the giant planet generates nearly twice as much energy as it receives from the Sun. So much total energy in fact that it would take the equivalent of 100 million large power plants on Earth to equal it. Scientists believe that Saturn's high energy output may be due to a combination of effects, including the release of energy left over from the planet's original formation, continuing gravitational contraction and the gradual separation of helium from hydrogen in the planet's core.

Saturn's Rings: Thousands of Surprises

Voyager's major revelations, though, turned out to be its surprising discoveries about Saturn's rings. Earthbound telescopic observations had long shown three rings (labeled A, B and C) around the planet, with a gap between the A and B rings called the Cassini Division. Pioneer 11 had discovered two more. However, Voyager quickly exploded the traditional view by revealing not the closely ordered simple structure expected but a complex and constantly changing system made up of *tens of thousands* of interacting ringlets! (See box on Saturn's rings.)

The "spoke" features in Saturn's rings appear in this Voyager photo

Voyager closeup of two of Saturn's major rings, the C-ring and B-ring

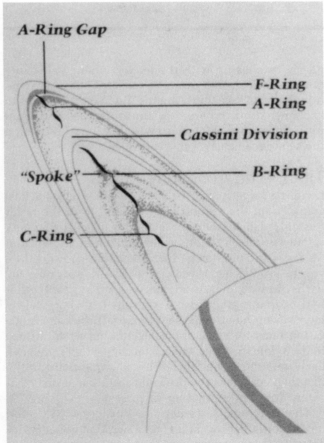

Diagram of Saturn's rings showing the major divisions

Nearly 249,000 miles (400,000 km) across and composed of millions of tiny particles of ice and snow, the fascinating series of ringlets sent scientists racing to their television monitors on Earth. What they observed was an incredible gravitational dance as ringlets interacted with ringlets and particles with particles. Although the Voyager cameras could only pick up the larger-scale activities of the ringlets, indirect evidence suggested other activities occurring on a smaller scale. The rings of Saturn in the new portrait offered by Voyager data were stunning indeed. The first major "stunner" was the discovery of what appeared to be "spokes" in the rings. Actually very tiny particles, about the size of specks of dust aligned in the radial direction but traveling with the movement of the rings, the "spokes" appear to be elevated just above the plane of the rings. Forming and dispersing within hours, the "spokes" still remain a mystery, although the best guess now is that the micron-size particles interacting with the rings are somehow kept suspended above the ring plane by electrostatic forces that may originate by interactions between the rings and Saturn's magnetic belts.

Another "stunner" was that some of the rings appeared not round but irregular, kinked in spots, and in one mysterious instance even appeared to be "braided"! To add further confusion to the picture, the major gaps between some of the rings suggested that something had "swept" those areas clean of particles. A best guess about the bizarre behavior in the rings was offered by the discovery of a pair of small satellites. Orbiting on either side of Saturn's so-called "F" ring these two small bodies, each only a few tens of kilometers in diameter, are thought to act like

Saturn's Major Satellites

Name	Diameter	Distance from Planet
Mimas	244 miles (392 km)	115,300 miles (185,600 km)
Enceladus	310 miles (500 km)	147,900 miles (238,040 km)
Tethys	659 miles (1,060 km)	183,100 miles (294,670 km)
Dione	696 miles (1,120 km)	234,500 miles (377,420 km)
Rhea	951 miles (1,530 km)	327,500 miles (527,100 km)
Titan	3,194 miles (5,140 km)	759,250 miles (1,221,860 km)
Hyperion	255 x 162 x 137 miles (410 x 260 x 220 km)	920,300 miles (1,481,000 km)
Iapetus	907 miles (1,460 km)	2,212,600 miles (3,560,800 km)
Phoebe	137 miles (220 km)	8,049,000 miles (12,954,000 km)

"shepherds" to the particles in the thin "F" ring, using their gravitational influence to keep the ring in its particular formation. If the theory is correct, then other similar small satellites interacting with the ring system may explain some of its other mysteries.

Saturn's Other Worlds

As Voyagers 1 and 2 took turns moving through the Saturn system, capturing photos and collecting data, scientists on Earth began to get exciting views of its remarkable collection of satellites. With 20 known moons in Saturn's system (and perhaps many more tiny companions yet to be discovered) the Voyager cameras and equipment were kept constantly busy. Ranging in size from the giant Titan down to small moons only a few kilometers across, most of Saturn's satellites orbit in an orderly fashion in the plane of Saturn's rings. One of Voyager's more curious discoveries was the fact that a few of those satellites, most notably Janus and Epimetheus, actually share a common orbit. These two tiny moons, each only a couple of kilometers in diameter, circle Saturn a few thousand miles outside its rings. Called "co-orbitals," the small satellites perform a curious ritual in which each takes turn following the other, their orbits only about 50 kilometers apart, until the trailing satellite

nearly catches up with the leader. Then, as the distance closes in this game of celestial "tag," gravitational effects take hold causing the two tiny moons to exchange orbits where they continue the game again until one nearly catches up with the other, repeating the sequence nearly four years later.

Titan: "The Atmospheric"

Looming large in Saturn's vast retinue of satellites, giant Titan, the second largest satellite in the Solar System, also loomed large in the interest of many scientists. Observations from Earth had shown that the icy world of Titan had an atmosphere. In addition, spectra studies had revealed the presence of methane, with infrared measurements suggesting that other hydrocarbons might also be present. In an icy satellite larger even than the planet Mercury these were interesting facts, offering some fascinating possibilities. Some scientists have speculated that Titan may have been home to some form of life at some point in the distant past. There was no doubt among scientists that Titan would present other surprises.

The first surprise came with Voyager 1. The good news for the "life on Titan" idea was that not only did Titan have an atmosphere, but the atmosphere was denser even than Earth's by about one and one-half

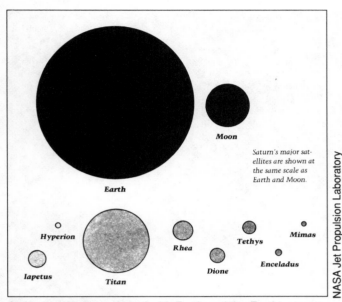

Saturn's major satellites are shown at the same scale as Earth and Moon.

Moon

Earth

Hyperion

Iapetus

Titan

Rhea

Dione

Tethys

Enceladus

Mimas

NASA Jet Propulsion Laboratory

Saturn's moons compared with Earth and the Earth's moon

times. More intriguing still, the bulk of the atmosphere was nitrogen, with methane only a minor constituent. Before Voyager, Earth itself was thought to be the only place in the Solar System with a primarily nitrogen atmosphere. In fact the nitrogen on Titan registered 10 times that of Earth. The bad news for finding out more was that chemical reactions in the thick atmosphere created a thick smog-like condition that made the surface of the planet invisible to Voyager's cameras.

The thickness of Titan's atmosphere also led scientists to downgrade their estimates of its size. A revised figure of just a little over 3,106 miles (5,000 km) for its diameter made it just slightly smaller than Jupiter's Ganymede, at 3,275 miles (5,270 km) in diameter—an impressive size, though, making Titan larger than the planets Mercury (3,031 miles, or 4,878 km, in diameter) and Pluto (probably about only 1,926 miles, or 3,100 km, in diameter).

Why should a giant "smog"-shrouded satellite be so interesting? The answer for scientists is in what might be going on both inside that "smog" and under it—on the surface of the satellite itself. Since Titan's atmosphere is primarily nitrogen, and nitrogen is a transparent gas, something else must be happening in the atmosphere to turn it into such a thick, shroud-like haze. The best guess is that since the atmosphere also contains methane and other elements such as carbon, oxygen and hydrogen, sunlight hitting the thick atmosphere could be creating some fascinating chemical reactions. The smog might very well be a

kind of organic haze. In many ways, in fact, some of those chemical reactions might be similar to reactions that occurred in the Earth's own atmosphere billions of years ago.

Is it possible, then, as some science-fiction books have speculated, that a kind of life could have formed on Titan? Although the possibility is intriguing, not many scientists are convinced. The extremely cold temperature, about −300 degrees F (−148.9 degrees C), stack the odds pretty heavily against it. Still, some interesting processes are taking place on the satellite's surface.

If the best educated guesses about the atmosphere are true, then some of the organic molecules produced in the "smog" may descend onto Titan's surface. The result could very well be a crust of organic sediment a kilometer or more thick. Since Titan is so large it may have also experienced some forms of internal geologic processes resulting in the formation of mountains, valleys and perhaps even some forms of volcanic activity. All would be covered by organic sediments. And since Titan's −300 degrees F surface temperature would allow methane to exist not only in its gaseous state but as liquid or water as well, liquid methane may rain down from the clouds, forming methane rivers and lakes, and methane icebergs may sprout near larger methane seas. Under its smoggy sunset, then, Titan may be a fascinating, cold and peculiar world indeed.

The Rest of Saturn's Family

Picking their way through Saturn's busy system, the two Voyager spacecraft offered waiting scientists a look at some of the other major members of the planet's family.

Like Jupiter's retinue, Saturn's satellites are mostly "dirty snowballs," icy worlds with varying amounts of rock.

The innermost of Saturn's major moons, *Mimas,* is composed of roughly 60% ice and 40% rock. About 242 miles (390 km) in diameter, Mimas's most striking feature is a gigantic crater just slightly off center on its leading hemisphere. Nearly 81 miles (130 km) in diameter and standing out boldly on Mimas's heavily cratered surface, the crater gives dramatic evidence to a collision in Mimas's past that must have come close to splitting the satellite in two. Mimas is also believed to share its orbit with one other small co-orbital.

Enceladus may be the most geologically active of Saturn's major satellites, and exhibits much more varied terrain. Like Mimas, Enceladus is composed mostly of water, with about 40% rock. With a

NASA Jet Propulsion Laboratory

This closeup of Saturn's moon Dione, taken at 100,665 miles (162,000 km), shows the many impact craters on its surface

diameter of roughly 310 miles (500 km), Enceladus has large areas of smooth plains as well as vast, apparently ancient, fields of impact craters. This satellite also shows some evidence of volcanic activity. The "lava" that may have erupted and blanketed portions of Enceladus's surface, though, would have actually been liquid water since the satellite's primary composition is water ice. One of the more intriguing features of Enceladus is that its surface is so bright that it reflects nearly 90% of the sunlight striking it. In order to achieve this striking reflectivity the surface of the satellite must be covered, scientists believe, with superfine crystals of ice which act something like the surface of a movie screen in reflecting light.

The most intriguing feature on *Tethys* is a large canyon or trench that stretches nearly three-quarters around the satellite's 659-mile (1,060-km) diameter. Estimates suggest an average width of 60 miles and depth of 3 miles, dwarfing the Earth's Grand Canyon by many miles in size and scale. Scientists' best theories about the origin of the canyon hold that it could have been created from the satellite's expan-

sion as its warm interior froze, or that it could be a giant fault through the entire planet due to the extreme brittleness of its ice. Like Enceladus, Tethys also shows a gigantic impact scar in the form of a large crater over 249 miles (400 km) in diameter. Tethys also shares its orbit with a large "family" of at least five much smaller "co-orbitals."

Moving outward from Tethys, *Dione*, like most of the other icy satellites in the Saturn system, also shows the scars of heavy bombardment. The largest crater on Dione is about 62 miles (100 km) in diameter. The satellite itself is estimated to be about 696 miles (1,120 km) in diameter and most of its surface is darker than the other moons in the Saturn system, indicating large regions of exposed rocks. The satellite shares an orbit with two and possibly three smaller "co-orbitals."

Rhea, with a diameter of 951 miles (1,530 km) is the second largest of Saturn's satellites. Its most interesting feature is a series of bright streaks crossing its face, which scientists believe may be caused by fresh ice or slush seeping out from beneath the satellite's surface.

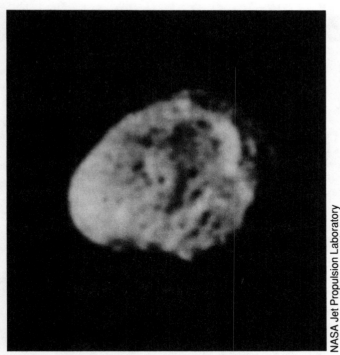

NASA Jet Propulsion Laboratory

Hyperion, Saturn's tiny irregularly shaped moon, is only 255 miles across at its widest point

One of the more unusual of Saturn's satellites, *Hyperion* has an irregular, elongated shape with diameter measurements of 255 x 162 x 137 miles (410 x 260 x 220 km) on its three axes. It also has a "chaotic" rotational rate, speeding up or down in an apparently random fashion. Although like the other members of Saturn's family it is a predominantly ice water world, it is comparatively dark and some scientists have suggested that its surface may have been contaminated by material from another object. These observations have also led some scientists to suggest that Hyperion may have collided with another body, perhaps a large meteorite, in its recent geological past.

Iapetus with a diameter of 907 miles (1,460 km) is also a satellite with a somewhat mysterious past. The third largest of Saturn's moons, it is distinguished by the extreme contrast between its two faces. The side of the satellite that leads in its orbit around Saturn is very much darker than its trailing side. An icy and heavily cratered satellite like most of the others in Saturn's system, Iapetus's darkened leading face has prompted some scientists to suggest a major deposit of material from an external source. Countering this "external source" theory, other scientists have speculated that the interior of the satellite may contain methane ice as well as water ice, which, seeping up to the surface, reacts with sunlight to become hydrocarbons, turning literally black as pitch.

Moving out of the Saturn system, Voyager also offered a glimpse of *Phoebe*, the outermost of Saturn's satellites. With its small 137-mile (220-km) diameter and retrograde orbital motion, tipped 150 degrees from Saturn's equatorial plane, Phoebe is believed to be a captured asteroid.

Mysteries Still Unsolved

As Voyagers 1 and 2 left the Saturn system in 1980 and 1981, they had performed their jobs magnificently. Peeling back its mysteries, they had answered many questions about the giant planet, its stunning rings and its intriguing family of satellites, providing Earth-bound scientists a new understanding of the planet and its family, a close-up look never achieved before.

The Voyager's visit, however, was short, and many mysteries are left to be unraveled. What internal processes actually occur at Saturn's core? Is our meager understanding of Saturn's atmospheric layers correct? How are rings around planets formed? Are our newly developed theories about "shepherding" satellites and their strange influence on Saturn's rings accurate? Could Titan offer clues about the origins of life?

Future Missions

Sadly, there are currently no further projects scheduled by NASA for a return to Saturn. If the USSR has any such project scheduled, it is still a closely held secret. With both nations' current emphasis on future missions to Mars, it is doubtful a Saturn mission will be considered seriously in the next few years, though many scientists would like to see such a mission on the drawing boards.

A possible joint venture called Cassini has been informally discussed by NASA and the European Space Agency (ESA). But Cassini at present has no funding, and some scientists think it would offer too little in the way of scientific returns in exchange for the money it would drain from other projects.

Many researchers would like to see a special mission to Titan that would probe its atmosphere and include a lander to allow close-up study of the satellite's mysterious and intriguing surface. Such a study might offer many rewarding clues to the mystery of life's origins here on Earth, and might uncover secrets still undreamed of on Titan's surface—perhaps even evidence of life. But at present, no such Titan mission is planned.

7

URANUS: THE FIRST OF THE LONELY PLANETS

At Jupiter and Saturn, we already had an idea of the general atmospheric circulation from Earth observations. But this is ground truth. This is original.
— Scientist at Voyager 2 press conference

A dull greenish ping-pong ball in the night sky, Uranus lies just beyond the range of Earth-bound observation. Like Neptune and Pluto, its fellow dwellers at the outer edge of the Solar System, Uranus's distance from Earth has kept it aloof and little understood.

Historical Uranus: Herschel's Planet

Unlike the planets that orbit closer to the Sun, Uranus is a neighbor whose presence was discovered relatively recently. First sighted by the astronomer William Herschel in 1781 and named for the father of Saturn in Greek mythology, Uranus for many years was known to astronomers as "Herschel's Planet." Orbiting around the Sun at a closest distance of 1,695,700,000 miles (2,735,000,000 km), it has a diameter of 32,116 miles (51,800 km), nearly four times that of the Earth. Uranus's most intriguing feature, though, was discovered in 1829: The planet is "tipped," with an axis sloped at 98 degrees. Unlike the Earth and other planets whose equatorial regions point toward the Sun, Uranus spins on its axis almost sideways, with its north and south poles alternately pointing "sunward." With an 84-year orbital period,

This photo of the crescent of Uranus was taken by Voyager 2 on January 25, 1986 at a distance of 600,000 miles

NASA Jet Propulsion Laboratory

66

Uranus: The Planet

Position: Seventh from Sun
Average Distance from Sun: 1,695.7 million miles (2,735 million km)—
    18.24 astronomical units (AU), compared to Earth's 1 AU, or 92.95
    million miles (149.59 million km)
Diameter: 32,116 miles (51,800 km), 4 times the size of Earth
Mass: 14.54 times Earth's
Density: 1.2 (Water = 1)
Volume: 64 times Earth's
Surface Gravity: 0.93 times Earth's
Period of Rotation on Axis: Once every .72 days
Revolution around Sun: Once every 84.01 Earth years (sidereal period)
Orbital Speed: 4.2 miles/sec (6.6 km/sec)
Satellites: 15, plus rings

each pole experiences 42 years of light followed by 42 years of darkness.

Prior to Voyager 2's visit to the Uranian system in January 1986, only five satellites were thought to accompany the planet in its long, lonely orbit.

Space-Age Uranus

Little more was known about Uranus before the space age. However, one of the more exciting discoveries about the planet was made, almost by accident, by a group of astronomers in an airplane in 1977, nearly nine years prior to arrival at the Uranian system of the first spacecraft.

The original plan was for astronomers flying on board NASA's specially equipped high-altitude aircraft, called the Kuiper Airborne Observatory, to turn their instruments toward Uranus as the planet passed in front of a distant star. Using this stellar-occultation technique (observation during the eclipse of a star), the researchers hoped to learn more about the planet's little-known physical properties. Fortunately they had turned their instruments on a half an hour before the occultation was to occur, and they noticed something strange. The light from the star behind Uranus dipped slightly *before* the planet passed in front of it! And it dipped again a half an hour *after* the occultation as the planet moved away! Had the astronomers discovered two new tiny satel-

lites, each one perfectly aligned on each side of the planet? No, the readings weren't leading in that direction. The other possibility—confirmed by telescopic observations made on the ground—was that Uranus had rings! Nine of them in fact! Much smaller than the rings of Saturn and much more indistinct, but rings nevertheless.

Voyager 2: The First to Uranus

Needless to say, the discovery of Uranus's rings had scientists waiting even more anxiously for Voyager 2's close-up look at the planet in January 1986. Splitting from its traveling companion after the successful Voyager 1 and 2 encounters with Saturn, Voyager 2 had been ingeniously redirected toward Uranus. As Voyager 1 headed out of the Solar System and toward dark space, its tour of duty finished, Voyager 2 found itself on another mission of exploration. It would take a quick run-through of the Uranus system like a camera-laden tourist making a quick stopover at an exotic port before moving on, but this "tourist" would capture images never seen before by the human eye.

Cameras and scientific equipment ready, Voyager 2 made its closest approach to Uranus on January 24, 1986, at a distance of some 50,000 miles (80,450 km). At that point the spacecraft was traveling 1.8 million miles (2.9 million km) from its home port, Earth, at nearly 45,000 miles (72,405 km) per hour. Even at that speed it had taken four years for the hearty little spacecraft to bridge the distance from Saturn to its new target.

Taking a Closer Look at the Rings

On examining the ring system, Voyager 2 quickly found two more rings to add to the nine already discovered. It also reaffirmed that the Uranian rings were indeed thin and somewhat tenuous. The innermost ring was about 10,000 miles (16,093 km) above Uranus's cloud tops and six of the rings averaged only 3 to 6 miles (4.8 to 9.6 km) in width, tiny in comparison to Saturn's gigantic and stately rings, which averaged *tens of thousands* of miles across! The three widest rings originally seen from the Kuiper Airborne Observatory averaged only slightly wider at 10-30 miles (16-48 km). Of the two newly discovered rings, one was narrow, in the 3-to-6-mile range, while the other proved to be the broadest of all, at 1,553 miles (2,500 km), but extremely diffuse—possibly a dust band.

An even bigger surprise was that the rings appeared to consist primarily of large chunks of almost coal-black material, on the average of 3 to 3,000 feet (.9 to 914 m) across, unlike the tiny particles that made up the bulk of the Saturnian ring system. In fact Uranus's rings contained few small particles at all! Some researchers think that the drag effects of Uranus's hydrogen-rich atmosphere may have pulled them down to the planet, leaving only the larger chunks undisturbed.

Why are the chunks black? The best guesses have proposed that the chunks are made of dark carbonaceous material or else have become contaminated by some kind of dark material, perhaps primordial, that is, made from substances that preexisted the formation of the Solar System. Or the chunks may be composed of methane ice that has blackened due to radiation effects caused by interaction with the Sun.

The Mysterious Magnetosphere

Still another curious mystery for the Voyager 2 scientists was Uranus's strange magnetic field. While most of the other planets in the Solar System have their magnetic fields more or less aligned with their rotation axis—as if an imaginary bar magnet ran through the planets from their north to south poles—Uranus's magnetic field is displaced nearly 55 degrees from its rotation axis. As the planet rotates along its axis, its offset magnetic field wobbles in space. To add even more complications to the picture, the solar wind arriving from the Sun and streaming past the planet draws the far side of the wobbling field into a gently elongated banana shape, an effect never observed anywhere else in the Solar System.

Uranus Itself

Taking a closer look at Uranus itself, Voyager 2 found an atmosphere composed primarily of hydrogen, nitrogen, carbon and oxygen, with a strange sheen of what may be ultraviolet light rising from the upper atmosphere. The entire planet is heavily shrouded in a smog-like haze and the temperature unexpectedly

The rings of Uranus, showing the "shepherd" moons, which orbit here in much the same way as the shepherd moons of Saturn's F-ring

NASA Jet Propulsion Laboratory

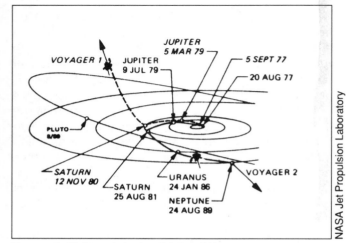

Voyager's flight path in the vicinity of Uranus

NASA Jet Propulsion Laboratory

Uranus's Major Satellites

Name	Diameter	Distance from Planet Center
Miranda	300.7 miles (484 km)	80,718 miles (129,900 km)
Ariel	720.8 miles (1,160 km)	118,623 miles (190,900 km)
Umbriel	739.5 miles (1,190 km)	165,289 miles (266,000 km)
Titania	1,000.4 miles (1,610 km)	271,112 miles (436,300 km)
Oberon	963.2 miles (1,550 km)	362,518 miles (583,400 km)

is almost uniform, varying little between the poles and equator. Voyager 2 also found very strong winds above the planet's surface, sometimes reaching as high as 200 miles (321.86 km) per hour, almost twice as high as the so-called "jet stream" on Earth. Although the Voyager 2 cameras couldn't penetrate the planet's thick smog, Uranus is almost certainly composed of ice with perhaps a small rocky core. Methane, ammonia and water are present and some climatologists theorize that below the heavy cloud cover may lie a deep, hot ocean of water and dissolved ammonia.

The First Look at the Uranian Satellites

Further fascinating surprises were in store for Voyager 2's Earth-bound crew of scientists when the spacecraft's cameras and instruments turned toward the Uranian satellites. In addition to the five previously known major satellites, Voyager discovered 10 more small ones with diameters of 50 miles (80.46 km) or less. It was the "big five," though, that drew the most scientific interest. Seen before from Earth only as tiny points of light, the five major satellites now became new worlds of wonder. Speeding through the Uranus system the Voyager 2 cameras and instruments couldn't linger long enough for prolonged study of Uranus's intriguing moons, but their quickly registered impressions gave scientists plenty to think about.

The innermost moon, *Miranda*, offered up yet another mystery. Only 300.7 miles (484 km) in

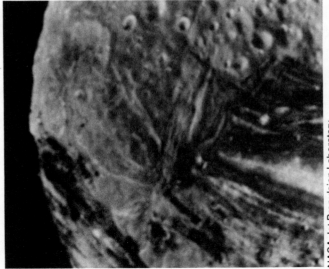

A high-resolution photo of Miranda, one of the moons of Uranus, taken by Voyager 2 at just 19,000 miles

NASA Jet Propulsion Laboratory

diameter it gave evidence of tremendous geological activity in its ancient past. Miranda showed two different kinds of terrain, one very old and heavily pockmarked with ancient craters, the other young and more complex, obviously the result of major geological changes. Deep grooves cut into the "younger" surface were visible, and strange racetrack-like patterns and rope-like imprints marred the surface. Most amazing of all on a moon of such a small size, a canyon 10 times deeper than Earth's Grand Canyon carved a path across its face.

Of the four others, *Ariel* also showed a young, complex surface, with wide, curving valleys and canyons. *Umbriel*, like Uranus's rings, displayed a dark surface, apparently the result of the moon's being overlaid by some kind of near-black material in its more recent past. *Titania* exhibited intriguing evidence of what may have been comet impacts occurring in the last 3 to 4 billion years. Light spray-like patterns also suggested that material from inside the moon had been ejected outward than fell back and froze on the surface. *Oberon*, like Miranda, showed evidence of enormous fault structures, including tall mountains and craters that appeared to have once been flooded with a dark fluid and then frozen over.

Mysteries Still Unresolved

Speeding out of the Uranian system in January 1986, Voyager 2 had again done its job well. As it headed toward its next assigned encounter, with Neptune in 1989, it left behind a wealth of information and more than a handful of new questions about Uranus, its rings and satellites.

Why is Uranus "tipped"? Why are its magnetic poles displaced? What causes the sheen of ultraviolet light dubbed "electroglow," in the upper atmosphere? Why are the rings dark, unlike Saturn's rings? Why are some of the satellites black? What happened to most of the small particles that must have existed at one time in Uranus's ring system? Is small Miranda so geologically active because of internal heating caused by the gravitational pulls of Uranus and the other Uranian satellites as some scientists suspect, or something else?

Upcoming Missions?

No new missions to Uranus are planned, and it is likely to be a very long time before humankind takes another close look at the planet. But Voyager 2 left scientists with a large legacy of information—volumes of photographs, charts and data still to be sifted through, studied and analyzed. The Uranus story is still unwritten, and it's likely that many more theories as well as surprises and questions lie ahead.

8

NEPTUNE AND PLUTO: THE DISTANT MYSTERIES

[A faint object was] . . . popping in and out of the background . . . as first one plate and then the second was visible through the eyepiece. "That's it!" I exclaimed to myself.

—Clyde Tombaugh
on discovering Pluto, February 18, 1930

All we can say is wow! What a way to leave the Solar System.

—Lawrence Soderblom
Voyager imaging scientist, August 1986,
during Voyager's last encounter, at Neptune

Far out in the Solar System, silently racing alone in the darkness toward its next destination, Voyager 2 nears Neptune. Cameras and equipment poised, the lonely spacecraft bristles with activity as it hurtles through space with one last job to do. Then, crossing over the invisible line that divides the known from the unknown, its journey continues. Leaving the human hands that made it far behind, its final duties done, its last messages sent, Voyager moves into a greater, vaster darkness.

The Search for "Planet X"

William Herschel's discovery of Uranus in 1781 had been an exciting event for planetary astronomy. Through his small telescope, Herschel had stretched the bounds of the known Solar System, and he had introduced not only a new planet to pique our curiosity, but also the possibility of still others. Noting an irregularity in the orbit of the new planet,

some scientists concluded that there must be at least one other large body beyond Uranus, influencing its orbital path.

The search for this mysterious body began haltingly at first when the mathematician John Couch Adams calculated its probable position and asked the Astronomer Royal of England, George Airy, to turn his telescope in that direction to verify his theory. Airy was indifferent to such a purely mathematical approach to astronomy and made no search. The French mathematician Urbain Leverrier met with similar resistance from his countrymen when he announced the result of his own calculations, and the discovery of Neptune was left to the German scientist J. G. Galle, who used Leverrier's calculations and discovered the planet in 1846.

A problem immediately arose, though, when it was soon discovered that Neptune, too, was moving along its orbit in an irregular way. Could there be yet

Neptune: The Planet

Position: Eighth from Sun
Average Distance from Sun: 2.8 billion miles (4.5 billion km)—
    30 astronomical units (AU), compared to Earth's 1 AU, or 92.95 million
    miles (149.59 million km)
Diameter: 30,858 miles (49,660 km), 3.89 times the size of Earth
Mass: 17.2 times Earth's
Density: 1.66 (Water = 1)
Volume: 42 times Earth's
Surface Gravity: 1.41 times Earth's
Period of Rotation on Axis: Once every 0.75 days
Revolution around Sun: Once every 164.83 Earth years (sidereal period)
Orbital Speed: 3.36 miles/sec (5.4 km/sec)
Satellites: 8

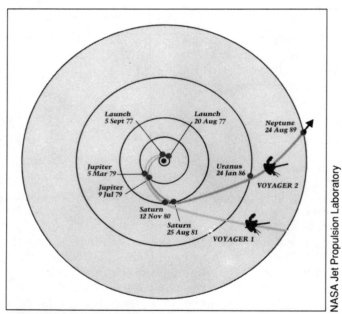

Voyager 2's flight path past Neptune

NASA Jet Propulsion Laboratory

With the failures of three of America's best-known astronomers, scientists in this country all but abandoned the search for "Planet X" for the next decade. However, in 1929, American astronomer Clyde Tombaugh finally did discover a planet beyond Neptune's orbit. An 11-year-old girl suggested the name Pluto (for the Roman god of the underworld, brother of Jupiter and Neptune), and the name stuck.

But was this new planet the mysterious "Planet X"? Maybe not. The problem was that this new discovery displayed an even more irregular orbit than the others—so irregular in fact that some astronomers insisted that it wasn't a planet at all but a giant comet or asteroid! Although soon accepted as a legitimate planetary body by most scientists, mysterious Pluto still remains an enigma. As a result, some scientists are still looking for a "Planet X" that would explain the irregularities in the Neptunian orbit.

Neptune: Voyager's Last Stop-Over

The eighth planet out from the Sun, Neptune has a nearly circular orbit, inclined 1.77 degrees from the ecliptic. At an average distance from the Sun of 2.8 billion miles, the planet takes nearly 165 years to complete its orbit. It is the fourth largest planet in the Solar System and at times (due to the eccentric shape of Pluto's orbit) it is the farthest from the Sun.

Although Neptune travels at a distance nearly a billion miles farther away from the Sun than Uranus, it is similar to its distant neighbor in many ways.

another planet outside of Neptune's orbit? A search began almost immediately for "Planet X" as this new and mysterious body was soon called. Intrigued, two of America's most famous astronomers, William Pickering and Percival Lowell, spent many hours at their telescopes during the first decade of the 20th century before eventually abandoning their quest. An exacting search by another American, Milton Humason, also failed in 1919.

NASA Ames Research Center

Giant antennas like these two at the Deep Space Network in California's Mojave Desert joined efforts with others all over the world to receive data from the Voyager encounter at Neptune

Nearly featureless as seen through Earth-bound telescopes, Neptune has a diameter of 30,900 miles, 3.8 times as large as Earth's, with a mass 17.2 times that of Earth. Neptune's atmosphere is mostly hydrogen with small amounts of helium and methane. It is probably the methane that gives the planet its slight bluish cast. Some scientists also believe that the methane, although slight, may affect the planet's balance of heat by absorbing sunlight. Earth-based measurements indicate that Neptune gives off more heat than it absorbs from the Sun. Some scientists think this excess heat may be caused by a release of energy as heavy molecules gradually sink toward the planet's core. Although most scientists think that Neptune has no solid surface, the density of the planet does suggest that it may have a small rocky interior with a mantle of water, methane and ammonia.

But when Voyager 2 swung past Neptune in August 1989 it changed forever the formerly faceless image of the great blue planet and its satellites. Before Voyager, only two of Neptune's satellites were known—Triton, which is about the size of Earth's

Moon, and Nereid, whose far-flung, eccentric orbit made it impossible for Voyager to photograph at high resolution. As early as June 1989, two months before arriving at the planet, Voyager had already found another satellite, a dark, icy moon larger than Nereid. Possibly not spherical, 1989 N1 (for want, at least for the moment, of a more imaginative name) was black as chimney soot probably due to a chemical reaction caused by radiation. Three more moons discovered on the inbound trip (1989 N2, 1989 N3 and 1989 N4) were joined by two very small moons (1989 N5 and 1989 N6), both less than 100 miles in diameter and orbiting at the inner boundary of Neptune's two rings. Voyager had found similar shepherding moons in the ring systems at both Saturn and Uranus.

As Voyager neared within 3,000 miles (4,800 km) of Neptune it rounded the planet's north pole traveling at a speed so great that on Earth it would have crossed the United States in just two minutes. Early in its approach to this great blue landless ball of gases, the spacecraft discovered an enormous storm system in its atmosphere, the Great Dark Spot, which extends

Pluto: The Planet

Position: Ninth from Sun
Average Distance from Sun: 3.7 billion miles (5.9 billion km), 39.44
  astronomical unites (AU)—compared to Earth's 1 AU, or 92.95
  million miles (149.59 million km)
Diameter: 1,926 miles (3,100 km), .24 times the size of Earth
Mass: 0.0035 times Earth's
Density: 0.7 (Water = 1)
Volume: 0.01 times Earth's ?
Surface Gravity: 0.20 times Earths ?
Period of Rotation on Axis: Once every 6.39 Earth days
Revolution around Sun: Once every 247.7 Earth years (sidereal period)
Orbital Speed: 2.92 miles/sec (4.7 km/sec)
Satellites: 1

over an area as large as the Earth. It is located at about the same latitude as Jupiter's Great Red Spot and its relative size is comparable. Whipped up by winds as fast as 450 miles per hour, the Great Dark Spot looks like a giant pod exploding at one end as it orbits the planet. It is just one of several enormous storm systems topped by higher-altitude clouds that scoot above them, but scientists are puzzled that Neptune could have such turbulent storm dynamics so far from the energy of the Sun.

Yet another major surprise discovered by Voyager was Neptune's rings, which from Earth observations appeared to be incomplete arcs. Neptune's great distance from the Earth, however, had made identification extremely difficult and Voyager established that though the rings are very faint, they do completely encircle the planet.

Probably the greatest excitement surrounding the Neptune encounter centered on Triton. Voyager passed within 24,000 miles of Triton just five hours after its closest encounter with Neptune. This mottled pink body appears to be the coldest place in the Solar System, at about 400 degrees below zero degrees Fahrenheit (both Pluto and Charon, which Voyager has not visited, appear from ground-based measurements to be warmer). It also appears to have volcanoes of ice, which may even still be active, blasting frozen nitrogen crystals as much as 15 miles up into the thin atmosphere. According to one scientist these volcanoes may be compared to geysers, but are actually unique in the Solar System. Triton also has a glowing aurora something like Earth's northern and southern

lights. It is caused by bombarding radiation trapped by Neptunian magnetic fields, the electrons from the planet's radiation belts (discovered to be present, much like the Earth's Van Allen belts) interacting with Triton's atmosphere.

Its last stop completed, Voyager sped on its path out of the Solar System toward the Milky Way. From its encounter with Neptune—and all the others before it—this small spacecraft leaves behind a wealth of information and images that will continue to yield new insights as scientists examine and analyze them in hundreds of different ways.

The Mystery of Pluto

Looking toward the Sun from Pluto, a future space traveler would see a small bright spot in the sky no larger than Jupiter appears to us from Earth. The ninth planet from the Sun at an average distance of 3.7 billion miles (6 billion km), Pluto may in fact be the last outpost in our Solar System. With its diameter of only around 1,000 miles (1,600 km), and a highly eccentric orbit that takes it to within 2,750 billion miles (4,425 billion km) of the Sun at its closest point and as far as 4,582 billion miles (7,375 billion km) at its farthest, some scientists have speculated that Pluto may not be a planet at all, but a comet, asteroid or even an escaped "moon" of Neptune!

Although we know little about the planet, it is believed to be composed mostly of water ice with a crust of methane. It was the discovery of this methane frost on Pluto's surface by Earth-based observations

Satellites of Neptune and Pluto

Name	Diameter	Distance from Planet Center
Neptune		
Triton	1,690 miles (2,720 km)	220,446 miles (354,765 km)
Nereid	211 miles (340 km)	3,425,949 miles (5,513,380 km)
1989 N1	261 miles (420 km)	73,075 miles (117,600 km)
1989 N2	124 miles (200 km)	45,734 miles (73,600 km)
1989 N3	87 miles (140 km)	32,623 miles (52,500 km)
1989 N4	99 miles (160 km)	38,526 miles (62,000 km)
1989 N5	56 miles (90 km)	31,069 miles (50,000 km)
1989 N6	31 miles (50 km)	29,950 miles (48,200 km)
Pluto		
Charon	398 miles (640 km)	11,806 miles (19,000 km)

made in 1976 that led scientists to downgrade their estimates of Pluto's size. The methane frost, they reasoned, would make the planet reflect more light from its surface, misleading astronomers into thinking that Pluto was larger than it actually was.

In 1978 Pluto offered yet another surprise when more Earth-based research led to the discovery of the planet's only satellite. Discovered by James W. Christy at the United States Naval Observatory, Charon has a diameter believed to be only around 398 miles (640 km). Orbiting Pluto once every 6.4 Earth days, only about 11,806 miles (19,000 km) from the planet's center, Charon probably has a mass around 10 percent of Pluto's, making the tiny satellite the most massive relative to its primary in the Solar System! Like Pluto, Charon is probably composed of water ice and methane, but, unlike Pluto's, its crust is almost entirely water ice.

Charon's discovery further helped to give scientists a more reliable estimate of Pluto's mass. As a result, astronomers realized Pluto couldn't be as large as some had speculated, ultimately leading to the present estimation of its size—around 1,926 miles (3,100 km) in diameter.

Farewell Voyager!
Leaving the Neptune system in mid-1989, Voyager heads outward to follow its companion spacecraft Voyager 1 out of the Solar System. What mysteries of Neptune it will have unraveled remains to be seen as mountains of its relayed data are studied and interpreted. Lonely Pluto, meanwhile, still awaits its first close-range inspection.

Will Voyager be the last spacecraft to probe the planets beyond the asteroid belt? Jupiter, Saturn, Uranus, Neptune and Pluto, like our closer neighbors Mercury, Venus and Mars, still hold many mysteries.

Only the future holds the answers.

PART 3

EXPLORING EARTH, ASTEROIDS, COMETS, THE CLOSEST STAR AND THE UNIVERSE

9

SOME PERSPECTIVES ON THE THIRD PLANET: EARTH

The poetry of Earth is never dead . . .
—John Keats

The Earth from here is a grand oasis in the big vastness of space.
—James Lovell, Apollo 8 astronaut speaking from lunar orbit

It swirls like a blue, green and white marble, this welcome oasis of a planet. Water sloshes its surface and the Sun's warmth spreads across it in a moderate and benevolent way. Its atmosphere, rich in nitrogen and oxygen, covers everything like a protective and nurturing blanket. Clouds group, drift and regroup in the atmosphere, hovering like watchful parents over the planet's teaming life-forms.

The intelligent life-forms called humans, one of the many living inhabitants, call this planet "Earth." It has become for them the standard against which all else in the universe is measured.

Earth: The Benevolent Planet

The third planet from the Sun, the Earth is the only planet presently known to support life. With a diameter of 7,926 miles (12,756 km), it is the largest of the inner, or "rocky," planets of the Solar System. It takes the Earth 365.2 Earth days to complete its orbit of the Sun, at a mean distance of 92,955,630 miles (149, 597,870 km). The Earth's rotation period is 23 hours, 56 minutes and 4 seconds.

Since the planet is inclined by 23.4 degrees to its axis, most of the Earth experiences a seasonal effect,

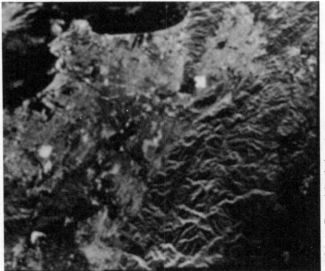

The L.A. Basin as seen from the Seasat satellite

NASA Jet Propulsion Laboratory

while the equatorial regions remain warm throughout the year. Although the North and South Poles have extreme seasons, they remain cold enough to retain

Earth: The Planet

Position: Third from Sun
Average Distance from Sun: 92.95 million miles (149.59 million km)—or
   1 astronomical unit (AU)
Diameter: 7,926 miles (12,756 km)
Mass: 13.2 x 10^{24} lb (5.98 x 10^{24} kg)
Density: 5.52 (Water = 1)
Volume: 1 E (Earth = 1)
Surface Gravity: 32.17 ft/sec^2 (9.78 m/sec^2), 1 E
Period of Rotation on Axis: Once every 23 hrs., 56 min., 4 sec.
Revolution around Sun: Once every 365.26 days (sidereal period)
Orbital Speed: 18.5 miles/sec (29.8 km/sec)
Satellites: 1 (natural)

permanent ice caps. Evidence suggests that dramatic changes in the Earth's inclination to its axis throughout its history have led to some startling changes in its climate, creating long cold periods called "ice ages."

The Earth has a solid surface, with nearly 70% presently covered by water. Ninety-six percent of this water is in the form of salty oceans. Earth is the only planet in the Solar System where water exists so abundantly in liquid form.

The maximum surface temperature recorded on Earth is 136 degrees F (58 degrees C), in Libya, North Africa. The minimum, −129 degrees F, recorded in Antarctica. The Earth's mean surface temperature is around 55.4 degrees F (13 degrees C), but varies greatly from area to area.

The atmosphere of the planet is nearly 120 miles thick and is composed primarily of nitrogen and oxygen. Scientists divide the atmosphere up into distinct layers roughly defined as the troposphere, the stratosphere, the mesosphere and the ionosphere. The troposphere is the layer closest to the surface, stretching upward about 7 miles (11.3 km). The stratosphere comprises the area from 7 to 30 miles (48.3 km) above the surface, the mesosphere, 30 to 50 miles (80.5 km), and the ionosphere, 50 to 150 miles (241.4 km).

Clouds are a permanent fixture in the Earth's atmosphere and from space they can be viewed in constant flux and movement over the planet's surface. Occurring primarily in the troposphere, the clouds are composed mostly of water vapor.

NASA

Cellular-type clouds above the Earth's surface as seen by the U.S. Space Shuttle 41-C mission crew aboard the orbiter *Challenger*, April 24, 1984

Internally the planet is believed to have a partially liquid nickel-iron core surrounded by a mantle some 1,800 miles thick. The mantle, which may be partially liquid, is composed mostly of magnesium and iron silicates. The temperature at the core is believed to be around 11,000 degrees F (6,093 degrees C). Some scientists believe that within the liquid core, the Earth may have a very small solid inner core about 200 miles (321.86 km) in diameter. As the planet rotates, currents in the molten iron in its interior are thought to be responsible for Earth's strong magnetic field. This magnetic field, in turn, interacts with the solar wind to form the Van Allen radiation belts around the planet.

The Earth's outer crust is thin, between 5 and 25 miles (8 to 40 km) thick, and is composed primarily of silicate rocks and some denser basaltic materials. The Earth is geologically active, with great portions of its relatively thin crust believed to "float" as large separate plates on the mantle. This effect, called continental drift, is believed to have slowly moved the planet's large continents around until they reached their present position. The presence of fault lines and earthquakes on the planet today give further evidence of the existence, boundaries and continuing movement of these plates.

Geologists also believe continental drift is responsible for many of the Earth's large mountain ranges such as the Alps and the Himalayas, created millions of years ago in the slow but relentless crash of gigantic moving plates. The tallest mountain on Earth, Mount Everest, reaches to 5.5 miles (8.85 km) above sea level and was probably formed in this way.

Hot molten rock from the mantle occasionally spews out lava in periodic volcanic eruptions—a process thought to be responsible for the creation of other large mountain ranges. Although not uncommon today, these eruptions were cyclically much more frequent in the Earth's past.

Life

The only planet in the Solar System known to support life, Earth has produced an incredible variety of forms. One million different living species of animals currently live on the planet Earth, and nearly 350,000 different species of plants. The complex, intelligent, land-dwelling and air-breathing vertebrates called humans have reached a worldwide population of over 5 billion.

Although this human population is distributed all around the land areas of the planet, it is densest in the temperate and near-temperate regions and is barely represented at all in the planet's icebound polar regions.

The presence of life on the planet has dramatically altered the Earth's surface by its creation of towns, cities, dams and other "artificial" structures.

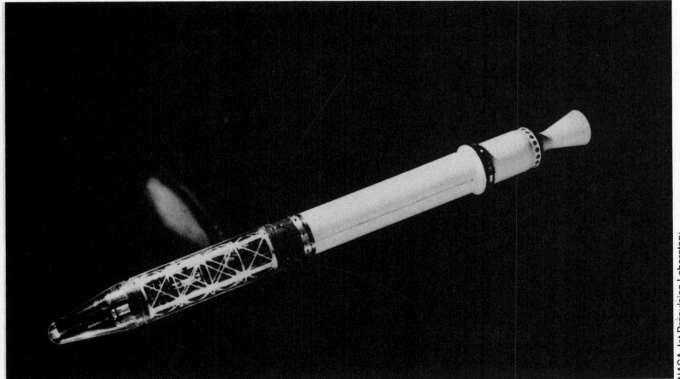

NASA Jet Propulsion Laboratory

A model of the Explorer 1 satellite launched January 31, 1958. The first U.S. satellite, Explorer 1 discovered the Van Allen radiation belts that surround the Earth

The Case of the Disappearing Ozone

The last half of the 20th century has seen a dramatic change in our view of Earth as bountiful and indestructible—a change brought about in part by the perspective we've gained by looking at Earth from space. One observation is the disappearance of ozone from the stratosphere.

Ozone has been an essential part of Earth's ecology for a billion years or more. Early in the planet's history, once plants began to contribute oxygen to the atmosphere, ozone also began to form through the interaction of solar energy and oxygen. As a result, an ozone (O_3) layer formed—a vast shield centered about 20 miles above the planet that protects terrestrial life from ultraviolet radiation that can be harmful, even lethal. Because ozone has begun to disappear, without its protection humans face increases in skin cancer and all life-forms will be seriously affected. In addition, due to related chemical reactions, the planet faces a general warming trend that may result in the melting of polar ice caps and widespread changes in agriculture and the balance of Earth's ecology.

Scientists first began to notice that ozone was disappearing from Earth's upper atmosphere in the 1970s, but by the mid-1980s the drama came to a sudden and unexpected head. From data reported by the Nimbus 7 weather satellite, scientists discovered that a huge, gaping hole in the ozone layer has been developing high in the skies over Antarctica each September and October since 1973.

By mid-1988 it became clear from investigations that one of the major culprits responsible for the disappearance of ozone in the upper atmosphere was a group of chemicals called chlorofluorocarbons (CFCs) used in refrigeration, aerosol sprays and styrofoam packaging. In a complicated chemical process, when these chemicals reach the upper atmosphere their components combine with ozone to form other substances. Hence the disappearance of ozone.

Under suspicion since the 1970s, CFC usage is finally being cut back— but scientists urge immediate action. As atmospheric chemist Joe Pinto puts it, "We can't go up there with vacuum cleaners, or pump up more ozone."

Strong evidence also indicates that certain chemical products created and used by humans have dramatically affected many of the Earth's land and water resources as well as the atmosphere, including the ozone layer high in the atmosphere, which protects the planet from harmful solar rays.

Space-Age Earth

Spacecraft originated on Earth have been sent out into the Solar System to probe the Sun, the planets and far-flung regions. Humans have sent robot visitors to seven of the eight other planets in orbit around Earth's Sun, and human explorers have walked upon Earth's satellite, the Moon.

Since the success of the first artificial satellite Sputnik 1, the Earth itself has been under almost constant observation by Earth-launched satellites. Although the vast majority of these have been utilized for military purposes, many others have been employed to study the Earth's environment and resources. Circling the globe in a variety of orbits, satellites have discovered the Earth's Van Allen radiation belt, tracked the movements of fish in the oceans, uncovered ancient lost cities in the jungles and roads in the deserts, monitored the growth of vegetation and the spread of pollution, aided navigation and revolutionized communications industries.

Quite literally the space age has changed the way humankind lives and views our planet and caused us to see ourselves in the context of the universe around us.

Mysteries Still Unsolved

While life has formed nowhere else that we know of in the universe, the secret of how life started here on Earth continues to elude us. Organic molecules suddenly may have begun to form from a primordial soup of methane, ammonia, hydrogen and water molecules in the oceans of early Earth. The first simple organic molecules (amino acids, proteins and fatty acids) may have formed in this soup, "energized" by solar radiation, lightning and possibly volcanic activity.

Or did it happen some other way? For instance, some evidence shows the basic structure may instead have been an inanimate clay that provided a template for more complex structures to form on, but, if so, no one knows where inorganic molecules crossed over to organic or why. The study of conditions on the other planets in our Solar System provides keys to understanding what may have happened some 450 million to 3 billion years ago when our planet was young and just beginning to teem with life.

But the origins of life question is just one of several. Beyond that beginning, we also know little about how more complex species evolved from early simple organisms and how humankind formed from the maze of other species.

And, our planet's future is also at question: Will Earth continue to be a place where life can survive? Or will war, pollutants and damaged resources spell disaster for this green and blue oasis in the blackness of space?

Future Missions

With the advent of the space age we've begun to extend ourselves beyond the confines of our own planet. The Soviets already maintain a permanent or nearly permanent manned presence in space in their Mir space station, launched in 1986 and hovering in orbit around Earth. This modular structure to which additional laboratories can be added has supported cosmonaut crews for missions up to a year at a time. Current U.S. plans call for building a space station called "Freedom" in cooperation with international

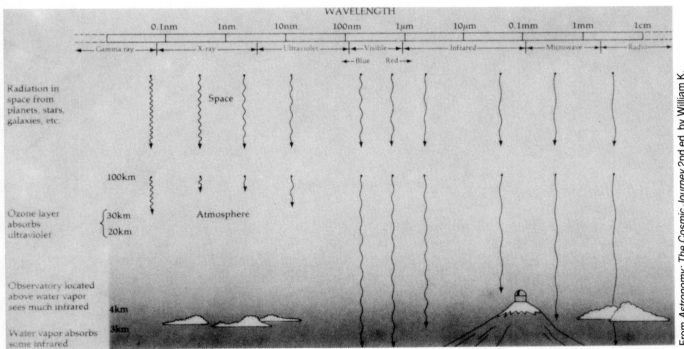

From Astronomy: The Cosmic Journey 2nd ed. by William K. Hartmann © 1982 by Wadsworth, Inc. Reprinted by permission of the publisher.

Electromagnetic radiation from space comes in many different wavelengths, ranging from very short (gamma rays, at left) to very long (radio waves, at right). Some radiation is blocked by Earth's atmosphere—for example, the ozone layer (located in the stratosphere at altitudes of 12–37 miles [20–60 km]) shields us from dangerous ultraviolet (UV) radiation from the Sun. Recent destruction of portions of this ozone "umbrella" has aroused worldwide concern

partners in the 1990s and early 21st century. "Frontier-type" colonies or bases on the Moon also figure in our thinking about space. And the distant future may see human expeditions to other planets such as Mars, and, perhaps someday beyond.

The intelligent inhabitants of Earth will continue to observe their own habitat, studying its resources and probing its potential. Watchful and concerned scientists worldwide have begun to join in an international "Mission to Planet Earth," combining satellite and ground-based observations of the planet's surface and atmosphere to measure how our environment is changing. The ever-increasing problems of pollution, the decreasing ozone layer (see box), destruction of forests, acid rain and the "greenhouse effect" are just a few of the global changes they are monitoring in these ways, hopeful that we can learn to improve the effects we have on our environment.

Increasingly sensitive military "spy" satellites also continue to proliferate, unfortunate symbols of the extension of war and human destruction into space.

Whether we use our intelligence and power to destroy or heal our planet, as custodians of our place in the universe the choice is ours.

Juniper's Great Red Spot, showing the turbulence of the upper layers of atmosphere

Voyager view of Saturn's rings

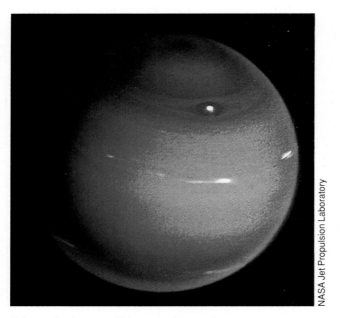

False-color image of Neptune. The red areas represent a
semitransparent haze covering the planet

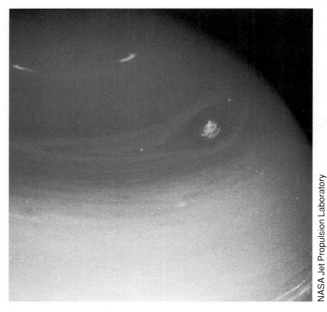

Cloud systems in Neptune's southern hemisphere

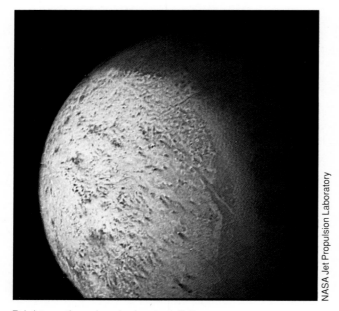

Bright southern hemisphere on Triton

Triton just after closest approach by Voyager

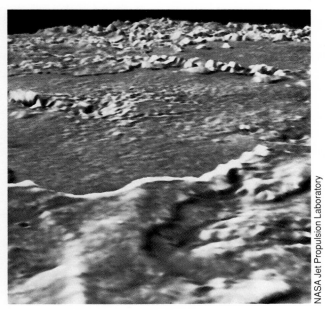

High-altitude cloud streaks in Neptune's atmosphere

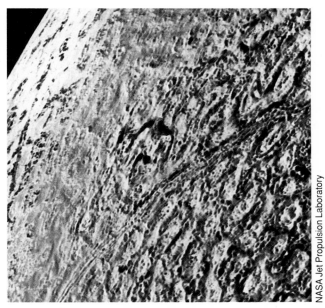

Triton from 80,000 miles. Depressions may be caused by melting and collapsing of icy surface

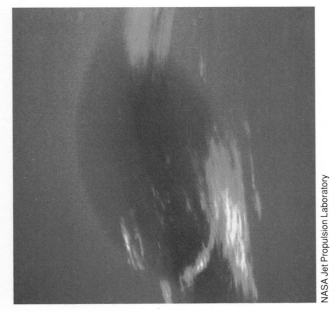

The Great Dark Spot of Neptune. This storm system rotates counterclockwise

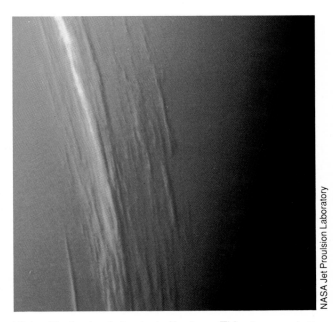

High-altitude cloud streaks in Neptune. This storm system rotates counterclockwise

NASA Jet Propulsion Laboratory

The "pizza-look" surface of Jupiter's moon Io. The massive volcanic eruption on the horizon is spewing debris 100 miles into space

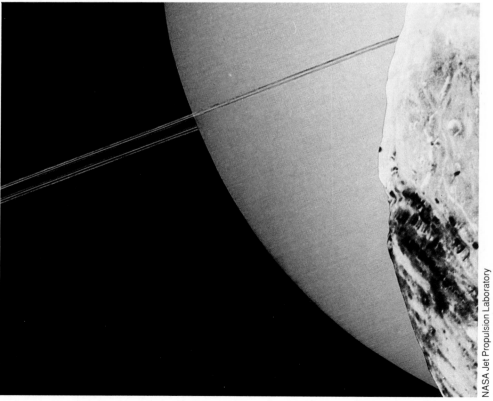

NASA Jet Propulsion Laboratory

Uranus and its ring as seen from 65,000 miles away over the horizon of Miranda, one of its moons (Voyager montage)

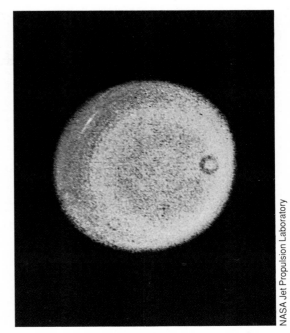

A false-color composite view of Uranus, as seen by
Voyager 2 on January 14, 1986 at a distance of 8.0
million miles

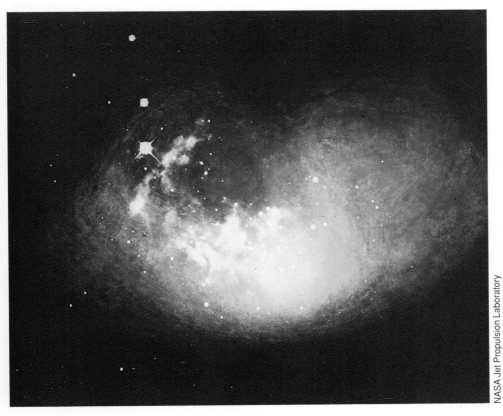

An infrared map of Orion nebula

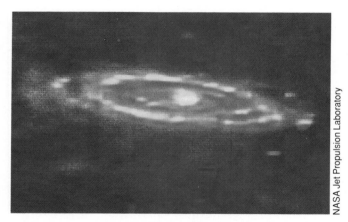

IRAS view of Andromeda galaxy. The bright yellow ring of clouds marks regions where star formation is occurring

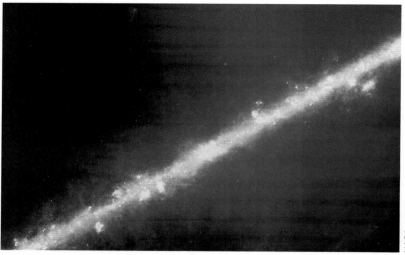

The center of our galaxy, as seen in the infrared by IRAS. (IRAS carried an infrared telescope that could see through the dust and gas that obscures the view through optical telescopes)

A newborn star called Barnard 5 (dark patch pointed out by arrow). This is possibly one of several protostars coalescing in this cloud. Our Sun probably looked much like this when it formed 4.6 billion years ago. Image produced from data collected by IRAS (Infrared Astronomical Satellite)

The giant planet Jupiter with two of its moons (Io, against Jupiter's disk, and Europa, on the right)

Hurricane Gladys as photographed by Apollo 7

Approach to Mars as seen by Viking 1

Earth, as viewed by the Apollo 17 crew on its way to the Moon

10

COMETS, METEORS AND ASTEROIDS: THE STRAYS OF THE SOLAR SYSTEM

Now slides the silent meteor on, and leaves
A shining furrow . . .

—Alfred, Lord Tennyson

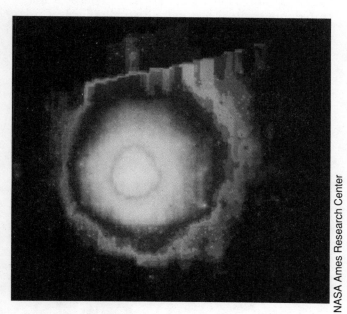

The coma of Halley's Comet, the cloud of gases surrounding the comet nucleus, as viewed in the ultraviolet by Pioneer Venus in February 1986

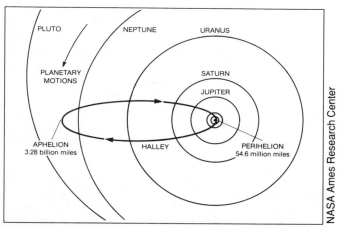

Halley's Comet moves in an elliptical orbit that reaches a distance of 3.28 billion miles (5.28 billion km) from the Sun, outside the orbit of Neptune (at aphelion or farthest from the Sun), to inside the orbit of Venus (perihelion or closest approach to the Sun). Other comets may originate from far beyond Pluto's orbit

They might be called the "leftover" pieces of the Solar System, these chunks of ice, metal and rock that we call comets, meteors and asteroids. In the great creation of Sun and planets they found no place; they formed no planet or satellite. They are the stuff of which our planets were made, the building blocks of the Solar System. And within their composition they doubtless still retain a multitude of 4.5-billion-year-old secrets, a wealth of primordial information, as they careen through space.

The Visitors of Vexation: Comets

In ancient history comets were thought of as portents of evil, marking the end of civilizations, the defeat of armies, and the deaths of rulers and great men. Today we know comets to be intriguing and natural products of nature, a part of the same process that created our Sun and Solar System.

No one knows for certain, but these "celestial fossils" may originate in the so-called "Oort Cloud" believed to extend a quarter of the way to the nearest star, or about one light year out (63,000 AU). This "cloud" (which may actually be a "shell" or hollow ring of material), may hold as many as a billion comets and is thought to have been created when the unused icy debris left over from the outer planet formation was "kicked outward" to fall into orbit, often far beyond the orbit of Pluto.

How do these comets then find their way to the inner Solar System? Although the exact mechanism is still unknown, scientists suspect that they may be "kicked" back out of the cloud by the gravitational effects of other nearby passing stars.

Whatever the origin of comets and whatever mechanism sends comets to beam spectacularly in Earthly skies, recent investigations by astronomers have told us much about their actual size and composition. Sometimes called "dirty snowballs," comets usually have a small nucleus composed of ices and solid particles—rocks and tarry organic material. Halley's Comet for instance has a nucleus only 9 miles long and 6 miles wide. This "solid center" is surrounded by a cloud of gases produced by evaporation of the icy nucleus—called a coma from which an ion "tail" develops as the comet approaches the Sun and interacts with the solar wind. It is sunlight reflected off the coma and the comet's ion and dust tails that create such a spectacular sight as the comet enters the inner Solar System. The "Great Comet" of 1811 displayed a coma with a diameter of 1.2 million miles, and a tail that stretched nearly 100 million miles long!

Comets fall into two categories—short-period and long-period—depending on the size of their eccentric elliptical orbits and the length of their orbital periods. Long-period comets may take many millions of years to complete their orbit around the Sun. Short-period comets, of which over 130 are now known, complete their orbits in much shorter times. Halley's Comet, perhaps the best known, returns to our skies once every 76 years, and the lesser known Encke's Comet completes its orbit in a little over three years.

Stones from the Sky: Meteors and Meteorites

Although the idea that stones fall from the sky may seem strange, a French physicist, J.B. Biot, proved by his careful scientific investigation into a meteorite fall near the French town of L'Aigle in 1803 that stones did in fact fall to Earth from the skies. These "stones," called meteorites, are actually meteoroids (interplanetary debris) that, because of their size and composition, have survived a fall to the surface. By contrast, the small, microscopic particles that burn up upon entering the atmosphere are loosely termed "meteors."

It is estimated that over 3,000 meteorites hit the Earth each year, most falling in deserts, oceans and remote uninhabited regions. Although most of these are quite small, the largest iron meteorite discovered

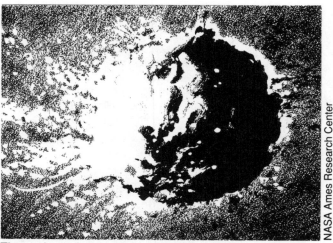

The nucleus of a comet releases a cloud of gas and dust as it draws near the Sun

NASA Ames Research Center

This meteorite found in Antarctica may have come from the Moon

NASA

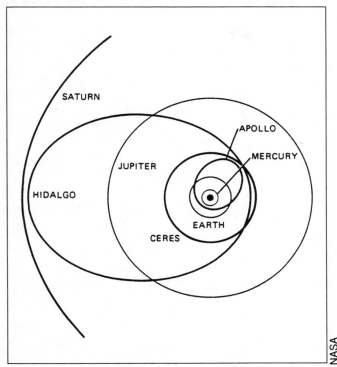

Paths of the asteroids Apollo, Ceres and Hidalgo

and photographic evidence gathered from the fireballs produced by small meteors as they burn up in the Earth's atmosphere substantiates that idea. There is evidence, though, that a few meteorites came from the Moon, and a few may have originated on Mars (although no one knows what the exact progress of their journey might have been).

Another group, called carbonaceous chondrites, are possibly parts of cometary nuclei. The enormous explosion that shook central Siberia on June 30, 1927 may have resulted from a hit from a cometary fragment. The event, called the Tunguska Explosion, left an area of over 25 miles completely devastated and there is some informed speculation that the meteor that probably caused the damage may have originated as a part of Encke's Comet.

"Meteor showers"—that spectacular display of fireballs at regular intervals that astronomy enthusiasts delight in—may also be related to comets and are believed to occur when the Earth passes through a stream of debris left in the path of decaying comets.

A Belt of Rocks and Metal: Asteroids

Like comets and meteors, asteroids are remnants of the planetesimals left over from the formation of the Solar System, but these orbit around the Sun much like a planet (whereas comets have far-flung orbits and meteors behave more erratically). In fact, asteroids are also known as "minor planets," rocky bodies that primarily orbit in a section of the Solar System called the asteroid belt lying between Mars and Jupiter. Smaller groupings of asteroids lie outside this belt, however, and about 1% of the known asteroids have orbits that cross the orbits of one or more planets. Two of these groups, called Apollo and Aten, for instance, cross the Earth's orbit. (Some scientists suspect that one of these Earth-crossing asteroids actually may have hit the Earth some 65 million years ago, spewing so much debris into the atmosphere by its impact that light from the Sun was dimmed for years, causing the gradual extinction of dinosaurs and some other prehistoric forms of Earth life. Although this theory is one of the splashier of recent years, it is still hotly contended and arguments for and against it continue to rage in scientific journals.)

There may be as many as 100,000 of these minor planets bright enough for eventual telescopic or space-faring discovery, but at present only 3,000 have been officially recognized. Of these 3,000 the largest

on Earth weighs over 60 tons, and the huge Barringer Crater in northeastern Arizona—over 3,900 feet (1,189 m) across and 600 feet (183 m) deep—gives ample evidence of the devastation such a fall can cause on Earth.

If we look at the battered and cratered surfaces of the other inner planets, we can see the almost mind-boggling effects of meteorite impacts in the early history of the Solar System. Like the comets in the outer Solar System, these meteorites are believed to be debris left over from the early formation of the planets. Unlike comets, though, which shared their icy characteristics with the outer planets, most meteorites were composed of the same solid material that went into the forming of the rocky inner planets. Most meteorites impacting on the Earth today are also made up of either rocks or iron and date back to the formation of the Solar System 4.5 billion years ago. They are scattered remnants of what was once a great deal of "leftover" planetary material called "planetesimals," now considerably thinned out by billions of years of impacts and the "sweeping" action of the solar wind.

Chemical analysis of meteorites found on Earth indicates that most of these objects originated as pieces broken off from asteroids. And observational

Missions to the Comets and Asteroids

Date	Sponsor	Objective	Spacecraft
1970	U.S.	Bennet	Orbiting Geophysical Observatory (OGO)
1970	U.S.	Tago-Sato Kosaka	Orbiting Astronomical Observatory (OAO-2)
1974	U.S.	Kohoutek	Skylab
1983	U.S., Netherlands, Great Britain	IRAS-Araki-Alcock	Infrared Astronomy Satellite (IRAS)
1984	U.S.	Encke	Pioneer Venus
1985	U.S.-Europe	Giacobini-Zinner	International Cometary Explorer (ICE)
1985-86	U.S.-Europe	Halley	ICE
1986	USSR	Halley	Vega-1 Venus (3/6/86)
1986	USSR	Halley	Vega-2 Venus (3/9/86)
1986	Japan	Halley	Sarigake (MS-T5) (3/8/86)
1986	Japan	Halley	Planet-A (3/8/86)
1986	Europe	Halley	Giotto (3/14/86)
1986	U.S.	Halley	Pioneer Venus
1989	U.S.	Asteroid ?	Galileo (possible asteroid flyby)
1991	U.S.-West Germany	Kopff or Wild-2	Comet Rendezvous-Asteroid Flyby (CRAF) (planned)
1990s?	USSR	Vesta	Mission to asteroid Vesta (tentative)

currently known is Ceres, with a diameter of about 633 miles (1,020 km). The smallest probably range down to something less than a mile! The most distant known asteroid, Chiron, has a diameter of between 60 and 200 miles (96.5 to 322 km). Some scientists speculate that Pluto itself may be an asteroid, once a satellite of Neptune. Some researchers also speculate that the two moons of Mars, Phobos and Deimos, may also be "captured" asteroids. Despite their numbers, however, the total mass of all of the known asteroids in the Solar System is probably less than 5% of the mass of the Earth's moon.

Present theory holds that most asteroids were probably formed when the gravity of the proto-planet Jupiter (early in its formation) prevented the asteroidal material from forming another full-scale planet nearby—leaving the majority of chunks in their present orbit and kicking still others out of the Solar System altogether or into their present planet-crossing paths.

Mysteries Still Unsolved

Are theories about the origin of comets, meteors and asteroids correct? Learning more about them can tell us more about the earliest days of our Solar System. How did the "Oort Cloud" originate? What caused the formation of the asteroid belt between Mars and Jupiter? Chiron's orbit around the planet Pluto is mysterious and it is unclear whether Pluto itself is an asteroid rather than a planet. Perhaps some dynamic event knocked Pluto away from an orbit in the asteroid belt or around Neptune. No one knows what mechanism may have shaken loose the small meteorites we have found on Earth that may have originated on Mars and the Moon. And controversy surrounds the theory that a collision between Earth

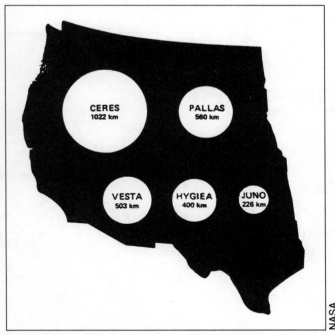

CERES
1022 km

PALLAS
560 km

VESTA
503 km

HYGIEA
400 km

JUNO
226 km

NASA

All five of the largest asteroids would fit easily within the western United States

and a comet may have caused the death of the dinosaurs.

Future Missions

There are not many observations of the comets and asteroids planned in our future. The United States's Galileo mission to Jupiter's major satellites, launched in 1989, may rendezvous with an asteroid and send back data on its way. A joint U.S.-West German project called the CRAF-Cassini mission (Comet Rendezvous-Asteroid Flyby) may get off the ground in the early 1990s. And the Soviets have talked of sending a mission to the asteroid Vesta in the 1990s. But, despite the view held by most planetary scientists that these ancient "building blocks" could reveal much of the early history of our Solar System, these explorations have not been given a high priority.

11

"SOL": OUR SUN

We started to explore the inside of a star; we soon find ourselves exploring the inside of an atom.
—Arthur Eddington, British astronomer and astrophysicist, 1824

It's a not-very-special, middle-aged star—lacking the dramatic status of its relatives, the red giants, white dwarfs and black holes. But to us it is the most important star on our horizon, this class G-2 star we call the Sun.

The Historical Sun

Although today scientists have a pretty good understanding of the Sun and its source of energy, ancient thinkers were primarily aware of its commanding presence in the sky and its obvious importance to the Earth. They thought of the Sun variously as a god, as a symbol of perfection and power, as a great ball of fire in the sky and as a vast blob of light conveniently placed by God for the benefit of mankind.

Sometime around 1507 the Polish astronomer Nicolaus Copernicus drew on his own and earlier work to advance the unpopular idea that the Sun was not only larger and more massive than the Earth but that the Earth and other planets actually orbited around it. Quite simply, the Earth was not the center of the universe. It was a shocking thought for the time. Today Copernicus is credited with beginning the scientific revolution, leading the way to the brilliant work of Isaac Newton a century and a half later, but the implications of Copernicus's work at the time were so disturbing that his classic book describing the Copernican System was actually banned by the Catholic Church until 1835.

In the early 1600s, however, Italian astronomer Galileo Galilei's studies and observations convinced him of the rightness of Copernicus's thinking. Galileo managed to provoke even greater anger when he announced his observation of sunspots on the Sun's surface (by then also seen by other astronomers), challenging also the prevailing view of the Sun's perfection. By observing the movements of these "dark spots," Galileo also proved that the Sun rotated around its axis once every 27 days.

The Space-Age Sun

The centerpiece around which all the planets revolve, the Sun is by far the most dominant feature in our immediate vicinity, holding 99.86% of all of the mass in our solar system. Compared to the Sun, Jupiter, Saturn and all of the inner and outer planets, moons, comets and asteroids are just lightweights, like moths fluttering around a street light. With a diameter of 865,000 miles (1.392 million km), the Sun is 10 times the size of Jupiter and over 109 times the size of the Earth.

Since the early 1960s the Sun and its immediate environment have been a continuing source of study by NASA and other world space programs. One of the earliest major studies by NASA was the Solar Observatory on Skylab (May 1973 to February 1974), where astronauts conducted experiments while orbiting the Earth in space. Using many sophisticated instruments

The Sun: Our Local Star

Spectral Type: G2 ("yellow" star)
Luminosity Class: V ("dwarf" star)
Position in Galaxy: 30,000 light years from the center, in a spiral arm
Age: 4.5 billion years
Diameter: 865,302 miles (1,392,530 km)—109 times Earth's
Mass: 4.385×10^{30} lb (1.9891×10^{30} kg)—333,000 times Earth's
Temperature (at center): 15,000,000 K
Distance from Earth: 92.96 million miles (149.7 million km)—1 astronomical unit (AU)

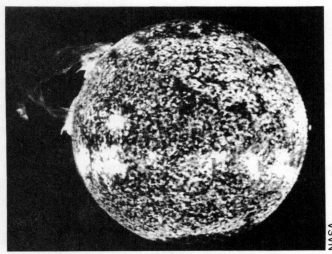

NASA

NASA's Skylab 4 mission crew took this extreme ultraviolet image of a spectacular solar flare spanning more than 367,000 miles (588,000 km) across the surface of the Sun

such as X-ray telescopes and an extreme ultraviolet spectroheliograph, they made measurements and took photographs of the Sun. Two continuously operating telescopes monitored the Sun and relayed television pictures to the crew. As a result they were able to collect a wealth of new solar information. A spectacular 150,000 exposures made by the instrumentation aboard Skylab during 1973 and 1974 represented a veritable full-scale assault on the Sun's mysteries.

Following Skylab, NASA's Solar Maximum Mission (Solar Max) satellite, launched in February 1980, concentrated on solar flare activity, while the continuing Orbiting Solar Observatories (OSO) program

running from 1962 to 1975, measured flares, scanned the solar disk and recorded fluctuations in corona and radiation intensity. Solar Max continued its observations until November 1989.

NASA, the European Space Agency, the USSR and Japan all continue to monitor our most important star and pursue its mysteries. Like our ancestors before us, we continue to view with awe, respect and immense curiosity the bright star that gives us warmth and light and keeps the world nestled comfortably within its small zone of habitability.

Today we know that the Sun is composed primarily of hydrogen and helium and is just one of many stars in the sky. Its average distance from the Earth is 92,955,630 miles (149,597,870 km), and its energy is generated by thermonuclear reactions deep within its core.

That core, which occupies 25% of the radius of the Sun and nearly 60% of its mass, has a temperature near its center of nearly 15 million degrees F (8.3 million degrees C) decreasing to around 13 million degrees F (7.22 million degrees C) at its outer edge.

Beyond the core is a large region or "envelope" that wraps around it and conveys energy outward toward the photosphere, the visible "surface" of the Sun. Not really a solid surface (since the Sun is just a giant gaseous sphere) the photosphere is several hundred miles thick. It can be thought of as an area of giant gaseous fire storms, appearing to us like tiny granules against the Sun's vastness and giving the Sun its mottled appearance. "Sun spots," first observed in Galileo's time, are believed to be cooler (and thus darker appearing) areas where localized magnetic fields seem to act as a suppressant to the normal flow of energy from the Sun's lower levels.

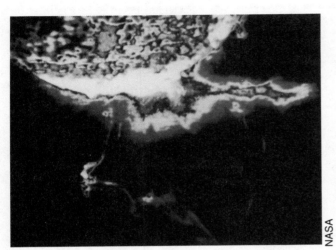

A Skylab extreme ultraviolet photo of a solar eruption

NASA

Outside the photosphere is the chromosphere, perhaps as little as 6,000 miles thick, merging into the corona, which we can't usually see. The corona is an immense field of hydrogen particles that extends for millions of kilometers outward into space where the solar wind carries a steady stream of energetically charged particles.

Mysteries Still Remaining: The Case of the Missing Neutrinos

Although our theories about the thermonuclear processes occurring deep within the heart of the Sun have been extensively studied and are almost certainly correct, one troubling problem still remains. A by-product of these thermonuclear reactions, tiny particles called neutrinos, with no charge and no mass, should be produced. Escaping in large numbers from the Sun, many of these neutrinos should shower the Earth where, although extremely evasive, they might be detected. But, how do you detect an almost ghostly particle that has no charge and no mass? In fact millions of neutrinos are believed to pass continually through the human body every minute without being felt or detected.

Beginning in the 1960s, scientists set up a complicated and extremely clever detecting device involving a gigantic vat holding 105,669 gallons (400,000 liters) of what is essentially cleaning fluid. The reasoning was that with the literally billions of neutrinos arriving on the Earth in an almost continual flow, an occasional stray neutrino should hit the contents of the vat where its interaction with a chlorine atom should transform it into an isotope of radioactive argon and this radioactive argon isotope could be detected.

While this did happen, the number of neutrinos detected fell far short of those predicated by our current theories. Was there something wrong with the experiment, or was there something wrong with the theory? As of today, the answer still remains uncertain. As attempts are made to refine and test our experiments to detect solar neutrinos, we remain faced with the troubling possibility that our theories about the thermonuclear processes of the Sun may be in doubt. If we're wrong about how the Sun works, then we will have to reevaluate all the ideas we have built upon our understanding of the Sun—extending outward to encompass all other stars, galaxies and the universe.

12

BEYOND THE SOLAR SYSTEM: OTHER STARS, OTHER GALAXIES AND THE UNIVERSE

The world began with what it is now the fashion to call the "Big Bang" . . . it could not, of course, have been a bang of any sort, with no atmosphere to conduct waves of sound, and no ears. It was something else, occurring in the most absolute silence we can imagine. It was the Great Light.
—Lewis Thomas
science writer

At the edge the new begins. The human mind is drawn to such frontiers. We have traveled to the edge of the atmosphere and into orbit, then to the Moon. We have sent probes ever outward, to observe Mars, Jupiter, Saturn, Uranus, Neptune, Pluto, other stars, galaxies and beyond.

What line is left to be crossed? Can the universe, too, have an edge? It is the nature of the human mind to seek answers. In such a quest there are always new boundaries, new frontiers.

Other Stars

Scientists have officially recognized over 100 billion, billion stars in the sky, and there are many more hundreds of billions to be discovered. The closest of these to us is our own Sun, at an average distance of 92,955,630 miles (149,957,870 km) away. The next closest is the triple star system called Alpha Centauri, 4.3 light years away. At that distance, light traveling at 186,000 miles a second would take over 4.3 years to get to us. If it were possible to drive a car to our own

Sun at an average speed of 55 miles an hour it would take us 193 years to get there. Driving that same car at that same speed to Alpha Centauri would take 52 million years! Obviously no one is going to travel 55 miles an hour to get a close-up look at Alpha Centauri (even if it were possible!)—not with modern sophisticated spacecraft available. But even popping a couple of astronauts into an Apollo spacecraft wouldn't quite do the trick since it would take them a little over 850,000 years to make the journey!

Science-fiction fantasies aside, it will be a long time before humanity ever sends a human or robot emissary to a foreign star system. Yet, scientists today know a great deal about stars. Using knowledge based upon our observations of our own Sun, and Earth and space-based studies of our Sun's "distant cousins," we believe we know how most stars are born, evolve and die.

Briefly, we know that, like our Sun, stars are powered by nuclear reactions taking place deep within their core. These reactions, primarily involv-

NASA/Hale Observatories

An optical view of the Andromeda Galaxy showing its elliptical nucleus

ing the conversion of hydrogen to helium, occur when the accumulated mass of a stellar body, or proto-star, becomes gravitationally great enough to trigger its nuclear furnace. Scientists believe that for the most part the original accumulation of that mass takes place under the urgency of gravitational attraction in dense and highly active concentrations of clouds of dust and molecular gas. Gravity is the key here. It is the unending "force" of gravity that first creates stars, triggers their nuclear reactions and determines the course of their evolution and eventual death.

To understand this it might be easiest to think of a star as being a great ball of gas, mostly hydrogen, at war with itself. It is this battle, between the star's gravitational contraction as its mass forces it to collapse inward (creating its nuclear fusion) and the outward thrust of energy generated by the tremendous power of this fusion, that keeps the star "burning" and determines the length and conditions of its lifetime.

The great variety of stars that populate space are simply stars of various sizes and masses at different stages of their lifetimes. The range of these masses is great, running from approximately 30,000 times

greater than the mass of the Earth in the case of smaller stars, to 10 million times the mass of the Earth with the largest ones. Depending upon its size and mass, each star will follow its own fate and meet its own ultimate destiny. Generally, though, a star of average size and mass, like our own Sun, will live to the ripe old age of 10 billion years before its nuclear fuel begins to run down. At that point, not quite ready to give up the fight for survival, it will begin to initiate other reactions causing it to bloat up to what's called the "Red Giant" stage, becoming so gigantic that its diameter would swallow up the Earth and everything on it.

Other less average stars will suffer other fates, ranging from a gradual quiet cooling in the case of less massive stars to the dramatic and explosively violent deaths of truly massive stars, resulting in "supernova" explosions.

These supernova explosions, among the most spectacular events in the universe, may leave behind in their wake tiny super-dense corpses called neutron stars. These tiny bodies have a mass so densely com-

The Hubble Space Telescope

Although the secrets of the universe continue to be pursued by Earth- and space-based observations (including such satellites as IRAS, the Infrared Astronomical Satellite, which operated for a year in 1983 and returned important data showing the existence of dust and gas rings around many stars), the Hubble Space Telescope will be humankind's greatest challenge to the mysteries of the universe.

Already built and scheduled for launch in 1990, the HST is the most sophisticated scientific satellite ever built. The telescope, named for astronomer Edwin Hubble, who first proved the existence of galaxies beyond the Milky Way, will allow humankind to see farther into the universe than ever before.

Plans currently call for the HST to be launched into orbit 378 nautical miles (512 km) above the Earth. By operating high above the Earth's atmosphere and free from the troubles that usually plague Earth-based telescopes, the HST with its 8-foot primary mirror will be able to view a much broader spectrum with much higher resolution than any existing optical instrument. With it, astronomers hope to be able to quite literally see back into time over 14 billion years and view objects born during the earliest days of the universe.

During its 20-year planned stay in space, the HST, with its ability to capture faint light sources equivalent to a firefly seen from 10,000 miles away, should also discover new phenomena never viewed before and may help unravel the mystery of the ultimate fate of the universe.

pressed that it can best be imagined by thinking of the entire volume of our Sun packed into an object with a radius of only 6 miles. A bottle cap of neutron star material would weigh over a billion tons!

Our Galaxy: The Milky Way

There are an incredible number of stars in our galaxy—over 200 billion. But, as galaxies go, it's not a very special one, except of course to us. Scientists estimate that there are over 100 billion galaxies in the universe, and over 30 billion of those are spiral galaxies like our own, the Milky Way.

Still, in mere human dimensions our galaxy's facts are staggering. Its 200 billion stars are scattered over an area over 480 million billion miles (80,000 light years) in diameter. If we could pack our entire Solar System into a tin can and put it into a vacant lot in the city of Chicago the rest of our galaxy would be the size of the entire continent of North America. Actually, our Sun and its planets are located around 30,000 light years from the galaxy's center.

Although looking up at the night sky with our unaided eye we perceive mostly individual stars, most stars actually come in double, triple and multiple star systems concentrated primarily in the galaxy's spiral arms. Many other stars in the galaxy are also found in clusters, called open clusters and globular clusters. Open clusters are believed by scientists to be young formations, only tens to hundreds of millions of years old. One of the best known of these, the Pleiades in the constellation Taurus, is thought to be only around 50 million years old. Open clusters vary in diameter from about 20 to 100 light years and may hold from a couple of dozen to several thousand stars.

The much larger globular clusters contain from hundreds of thousands to several millions of stars. The galaxy appears to contain about 300 globular clusters and these clusters are much older and more stable than the open clusters, containing aging stars that may have existed since the galaxy's beginning.

European Space Agency

An artist's concept of the Hubble Space Telescope in orbit

As a whole, then, our galaxy is a gigantic, flattened and spiral-shaped gravitationally bound collection of stars (and very likely, at least some other solar systems including planets and planetary debris), clusters of stars, nebulae (dense areas of gas and dust "clouds" where new stars may be forming), and a huge amount of free interstellar gas and dust.

Other Galaxies

Based upon observations, scientists categorize galaxies into three roughly basic shapes, the spiral galaxies like our own Milky Way, elliptical galaxies and irregular galaxies. The spirals make up about 30% of the estimated 100 billion galaxies in the universe, the ellipticals (the most commonly found) around 60%, and irregular galaxies somewhere around 10%.

The spiral galaxies are less massive but brighter than the ellipticals, and are thought to be much younger. Their stellar population is composed primarily of hot, young blue stars that dominate the spiral arms, and they are filled with clouds of interstellar gas and dust where new stars are obviously being born.

The elliptical galaxies, while more massive, are much dimmer and cooler—and so probably much older. Old red stars dominate the stellar population of these galaxies. The ellipticals contain little interstellar gas and dust and there is no evidence of new star formation.

Irregular galaxies are much fewer in number and, as the name implies, come in a variety of shapes. The irregulars are also much smaller and contain large amounts of interstellar matter.

Like stars, galaxies rarely exist as single isolated units. They are much more likely to come in pairs, triplets or even larger systems. The small group of which the Milky Way is a part contains about 25 galaxies. Called the Local Group by astonomers, the entire group stretches to encompass an area about 3 million light years in diameter.

The nearest galaxies to our own Milky Way in this group are the Large Magellanic Cloud at about 160,000 light years away and the Small Magellanic Cloud around 185,000 light years away. Our next-door neighbors are situated in our sky in such a way, though, that they can only be viewed in the Southern Hemisphere or by space-based observations. Although most scientists believe that the Magellanic Clouds are small, irregular galaxies, a few others think that they have seen a faint spiral structure in our distant companions.

The Universe

It would be wrong to think of the universe as simply the container of everything—galaxies, stars, solar systems, interstellar and interplanetary matter, and so on. The idea of a container implies the existence of something outside the container. Planets are part of a solar system, stars a part of a galaxy, galaxies a part of the universe, the universe a part of a . . . what? It's difficult for the human mind to imagine an *all* that is in itself *all* and for which there is not even a beyond or an "outside of."

And yet when scientists speak of the universe they speak of *all* space, and *all* time. Although scientists refer to the universe as coming into being about 18 billion years ago in a spectacular event called the Big Bang, it might be more appropriate to say that "being came into being" with that occurrence. For we cannot say that there was a "before that time," since, as difficult as it is to imagine, there was no "before" and no "time"!

The Big Bang (an event that is a part of the presently most popular, most accepted and partially proven theory about the origin of the universe) is believed by scientists to have occurred 18 billion years ago. It is perhaps easiest, although in some ways incorrect, to think of it as a gigantic explosion—literally inconceivable in its magnitude. In the beginning, scientists believe, energy was packed into an inconceivably small point at a virtually infinite temperature. At some moment, though, in a hundred million billionths of a second, after "the event" all the matter and energy of the universe existed in its entirety in some unknown form in a dimension smaller than a single atomic nucleus! And then suddenly, quicker than the mind can easily comprehend and occurring in unbelievably short time spans that scientists talk of as trillionths and billionths of a single second, the universe expanded to the size of a beach ball then to the size of our Solar System—and quickly beyond. During this period the initial energy released in the Big Bang went through a series of transformations as the universe continued to expand and cool.

By the end of the first minute all of the known particles and forces that scientists understand today had come into existence. By the time the universe was around two minutes old and its temperature had fallen to about a billion degrees, these particles had begun to combine to form the nuclei of hydrogen and helium atoms.

Continuing to expand and cool, the process would take several hundred thousand years, though, before the cooling would reach a temperature that would allow the nuclei to join with electrons to form hydrogen and helium atoms. But once this step had occurred, somehow in a process still little understood, the resultant gas became "clumped" enough for the force of gravity to begin the process of individual star-building.

With the formation, evolution and death of those first stars and galaxies of stars came the universe as we know it today.

For it was within the tremendous furnace of the stars that the simple elements of hydrogen and helium were forged together to create the larger atoms that became the stuff of life and everything else. It is more than a poetic thought to say that human life, as well as most everything that we live with each day, is made of "stardust."

The universe is still expanding today. We are all still quite literally caught up in the cosmic "explosion" begun 18 billion years ago. Astronomers observe daily evidence that the galaxies including our own are, for the most part, moving away from one another, a picture that if reversed would bring them all together at a single point in time and space.

We know also that the temperature that once began infinitely high has now cooled with the universe's continued expansion to its present 3 degrees Kelvin, or −454 degrees F (−270 degrees C). This temperature is caused by cosmic background radiation, a cumulative radiation from many unresolved, individually weak sources that emit radio waves, x-rays and so on. It was the discovery of this background radiation, first detected in the form of microwaves in 1964 but previously predicted by Big Bang theorists, combined with evidence of the universe's uniform expansion, that finally persuaded many scientists of the validity of the Big Bang theory.

The Biggest Mystery of Them All

How will it all end? Will the universe continue to expand and cool, and if so what will be its eventual fate? Or will it stop expanding someday? Scientists believe that there is some evidence that the expansion is slowing down as the gravitational tug of each object in the universe acts upon each other object to resist the expansion. Are there enough "objects"; is there enough "mass" to stop the expansion completely? Is it a Closed Universe that will expand and then shrink back to begin over again, as some scientists think, or is it an Open Universe that will expand forever?

So far, our best calculations say that much more mass would be required to stop the expansion than we have yet discovered. Is there more mass yet to be discovered?

What would be the fate of a universe that continues to expand? Scientists believe that such a universe would undergo a "heat death," a long drawn-out terminal equilibrium in which *all* the stars and galaxies would eventually burn out and all matter would decay.

In a much more dramatic and explosive finale, scientists believe a Closed Universe would collapse inward on itself. Just as the galaxies now race apart from one another, they would eventually reverse their movement to all be drawn violently—like a motion picture running crazily backward—toward a single point in space, returning with a cataclysmic squashing of galaxies, stars, planets and all matter into a final annihilating "big crunch"!

And then . . .? Will the universe experience another Big Bang to repeat the process all over?

No one knows today what the answers are to these questions, and certainly knowing them will not affect the outcome of the universe and its ultimate fate. But asking questions like these and seeking the answers is the most human of activities. As long as humanity continues to exist it will continue to ask questions, postulate answers, test and examine them, and then ask more questions, in a continual process of trying to understand.

GLOSSARY

accrete (v.) To grow by being added to.

accretion Growth in size through addition or accumulation.

asteroid A small remnant of the planetesimals left over from formation of the Solar System.

astronomical unit (AU) Distance from Earth to the Sun (92.95 million miles [149.59 million km])

binary star A double star or two-star system with two stars revolving around a common center of gravity.

booster A rocket system that launches a spacecraft or other payload; also, any one of the early stages of a multistage rocket.

carbonaceous chondrite A type of meteorite rich in carbon and volatile elements, thought to be among the earliest-formed unaltered objects in the Solar System.

charged particle A particle that is not electrically neutral, that is, carries an electrical charge, either negative (an electron, for example) or positive (a proton).

chromosphere A reddish-colored layer in the Sun's atmosphere, just outside the photosphere. Perhaps 6,000 miles thick, it merges into the outermost area of the Sun, the corona.

coma The diffuse area around the nucleus of a comet; the two together form the comet's head.

comet A small interplanetary object made largely of ice and dust. As a comet orbits about the Sun it becomes heated during its passage through the inner Solar System, giving off gases that are visible as a glowing, diffuse nucleus with a long tail.

continental drift The movement of continents due to motion beneath them of material in a planet's mantle.

convection A flow of mass that moves hot material into cooler regions, or cool material into hotter regions, transporting heat from one location to another.

corona The outermost region of the Sun's atmosphere, an immense field of hydrogen particles, extending millions of miles outward into space and invisible to the naked eye.

cosmic rays High-energy atomic particles in space, many originating in supernovas and pulsars.

decay Spontaneous radioactive disintegration.

disk A plate-shaped object, such as the image of the full Moon seen in the sky (a term from observational astronomy).

electron A small particle carrying a negative electrical charge; it balances the charge of the proton and with the neutron, makes an atom.

elliptical In the shape of a squashed circle—an oval.

elliptical galaxy A grouping of stars appearing to have an oval shape in observation—about 60% of the galaxies in the universe.

European Space Agency (ESA) A collaborative agency formed by several European countries for the purpose of launching satellites and exploring space.

flyby A space mission designed to observe its objective, such as the Sun or a planet, by flying past, rather than orbiting it or landing on it.

galaxy A large grouping of millions to hundreds of billions of stars.

gamma rays A type of radiation having extremely short wavelengths (shorter even than ultraviolet and x-rays) that are not visible and do not penetrate the Earth's atmosphere.

gravitational attraction The force by which one mass attracts another.

gravity assist The use of the gravitational force of a body in space to assist a spacecraft on its voyage. Used, for example, by Mariner 10 to gain power to complete its trip to Mercury.

heliosphere The region into which the solar wind (the flow of energetic charged particles from the Sun's corona outward into space) expands.

infrared radiation Radiation with wavelengths beyond the red end of the visible spectrum.

ionosphere The outermost portion of the Earth's atmosphere, stretching from 50 to 150 miles (80.5 to 241.4 km) above the surface.

irregular galaxy One of the three main types of galaxies, irregular in shape, making up about 10% of all galaxies in the universe.

isotope A relative of an element that has the same number of protons, but a different number of neutrons in its nucleus than its cousin element.

Kelvin A system of temperature measurement commonly used in astronomy. 0° Kelvin is absolute zero, the point at which a substance would have no molecular motion and no heat (−273° C or −459.67° F).

leading (as in hemisphere) The portion of a planet or moon's disk that is seen first in observation.

light minute The distance light travels in one minute (11,160,000 miles, about 18 million km).

light year One light year (about 6 trillion miles or 9.7 million km) is the distance light travels in one year, at the speed of 186,000 miles a second. For example the closest star in the universe (aside from the Sun) is Proxima Centauri, at a distance of over 25 trillion miles or 4.3 light years.

magnetometer An instrument to measure a magnetic field.

mare (pl. maria) Dark, smooth areas (such as those on the Moon and Mercury) that look like seas from a distance.

mass The property of a body that causes it to have weight in a gravitational field; material or the amount of material.

mesosphere The layer of Earth's atmosphere located at an altitude of 30 to 50 miles (48.3 to 80.5 km), between the stratosphere and the ionosphere.

meteorite A small interplanetary object that lands on Earth.

meteoroid A small interplanetary object, usually only a few yards or meters across, or smaller.

microwave Electromagnetic waves with wavelengths near 1 centimeter.

nebula A cloud of interstellar gas and dust.

neutrino Very small particles having no charge and no mass, believed to travel at the speed of light.

noble gas A chemically unreactive gas (will not combine with other elements), such as helium and neon.

nuclear fusion The same principle used by the hydrogen bomb—in which the nuclei of lightweight atoms, such as deuterium or tritium, fuse to form a nucleus of heavier mass such as helium. Because the combined mass is smaller, energy is released.

orbital revolution Motion of one body around another, such as the orbit of a planet around the Sun.

orbiter A spacecraft designed to observe by orbiting around its objective.

payload The cargo carried by a spacecraft.

photosphere The visible "surface" of the Sun, several kilometers thick, an area of giant gaseous fire storms.

pixel The individual portions into which an image is divided, short for picture element.

plane A term from geometry. A surface that wholly contains every straight line joining any two points lying in it. Objects located in the plane of a disk would be located anywhere along a radius of the disk.

proton A charged particle (with a positive charge), found in the nucleus of an atom.

radiation The process of sending out rays of energy in the form of heat, light and so on.

radioactive Describes an element (such as uranium) whose nucleus disintegrates spontaneously.

radiometry Use of a device that measures the total energy output from a body in the form of radiation.

resolution The degree to which an image shows fine details.

retrograde Revolution or rotation from east to west (not the usual direction found in the Solar System).

retrorocket A rocket that fires against the movement of a spacecraft to slow or reverse direction.

rift valley A valley formed by a large crack in the crust of a planet.

rotation Motion of a body around its own internal axis.

soft landing A landing that sets the spacecraft down gently, without harm to its contents.

solar cell A device that converts solar radiation into electrical energy.

solar wind The flow of charged particles streaming outward from the Sun's corona at supersonic speeds.

spectrum (pl., spectra) A display of colors or intensities produced by a source of electromagnetic radiation, organized in the order of wavelength or frequency.

spectroscopy The production and study of spectra.

spiral galaxy A galaxy that appears to have spiral arms, like our own galaxy, the Milky Way. This type of galaxy makes up about 30% of the estimated 100 billion galaxies in the universe.

stellar occultation The apparent disappearance of a star when another body (such as the disk of the Moon or a planet) passes in front of it and hides it either completely or partially from view. Extensive astronomical information can be obtained by measuring the precise timings of occultations.

stratosphere The portion of the Earth's atmosphere stretching upward from 7 to 30 miles (11.3 to 48.3 km) above the surface, above the troposphere.

supernova Stellar explosion—an extremely bright nova with sudden increase of 10 million to 100 million times in brightness, blowing off most of a star's mass and leaving a dense core.

tectonic Relating to changes in a planet's crust, especially large-scale movements.

thermonuclear reaction A reaction in which isotopes of a light element (such as deuterium and tritium, isotopes of hydrogen), fuse at very high temperatures into heavier nuclei (such as helium), giving off energy.

torus A donut shape.

trace element Any element present in minute quantities.

trajectory The curved path followed by a projectile, such as a spacecraft.

troposphere The layer of atmosphere closest to the Earth (the air we breathe), stretching upward from the surface to about 7 miles (11.3 km).

ultraviolet (UV) Radiation having a wavelength too short to see, beyond the blue end of the visible spectrum, but longer than x-rays and gamma rays. Most ultraviolet rays do not penetrate Earth's atmosphere.

ultraviolet spectrometer An instrument for recording the spectrum of radiation at ultraviolet wavelengths.

volatile A substance that evaporates readily, such as water, methane and ammonia (as opposed to non-volatile substances such as iron and silicates).

wavelength In the wavelike characteristic of electromagnetic radiation, the distance between two peaks or between two valleys in a wave.

x-band One of two radio frequencies used in communication with interplanetary spacecraft. More economical but less accurate, it is used primarily for less sensitive data.

x-ray Electromagnetic radiation of the same type as light but with extremely short wavelengths, between ultraviolet and gamma rays on the spectrum. Like UV and gamma rays, x-rays are not visible.

SUGGESTIONS FOR FURTHER READING

Books

Burgess, Eric. *To the Red Planet.* New York: Columbia University Press, 1978.

Cadogan, P. *The Moon: Our Sister Planet.* New York: Cambridge University Press, 1981.

Carr, Michael H. *The Surface of Mars.* New Haven, CT: Yale University Press, 1981.

Cooper, Henry S. F., Jr. *The Search for Life on Mars: Evolution of an Idea.* New York: Holt, Rinehart and Winston, 1980.

Donne, J. and E. Burgess. *The Voyage of Mariner 10.* NASA Special Publication 424, 1978.

Fimmel, Richard, *et al. Pioneer: First to Jupiter, Saturn, and Beyond.* NASA Special Publication 446, 1980.

————. *Pioneer Odyssey.* NASA Special Publication 396, 1977.

————. *Pioneer Venus.* NASA Special Publication 461, 1982.

Hartmann, William K. *Astronomy: The Cosmic Journey*, Fourth Edition. Belmont, CA: Wadsworth, 1989.

Hunt, G. and P. Moore. *The Planet Venus.* Winchester, MA: Faber and Faber, 1982.

Hutchinson, R. *The Search for Our Beginnings.* New York: Oxford University Press, 1983.

Moore, Patrick, ed. *The International Encyclopedia of Astronomy.* West Brattleboro, VT: Orion Books, 1987.

Morrison, D. *Voyages to Saturn.* NASA Special Publication 451, 1982.

————, and J. Samz. *Voyage to Jupiter.* NASA Special Publication 439, 1980.

Preiss, Byron, ed. *The Planets.* New York: Bantam Books, 1985.

Sagan, Carl. *Cosmos.* New York: Random House, 1980.

For further reading on space exploration, the following publications offer the most up-to-date information, and most are available at school and public libraries and larger bookstores:

Ad Astra (published by the National Space Society)

Astronomy

Aviation Week and Space Technology

Discover

Final Frontier

Mercury (published by the Astronomical Society of the Pacific)

National Geographic Magazine

Planetary Report (published by the Planetary Society)

Popular Science

Science News

Scientific American

INDEX